FOR ORGANS, PIANOS & ELECTRONIC KEYBOARDS

E-Z PLAY TODAY

128

JOHN WILLIAMS

T0084261

ISBN 978-1-4803-2984-3

HAL•LEONARD®
CORPORATION

7777 W. BLUEMOUND RD. P.O. BOX 13819 MILWAUKEE, WI 53213

Visit Hal Leonard Online at
www.halleonard.com

Across the Stars

Love Theme from STAR WARS: EPISODE II – ATTACK OF THE CLONES

Registration 1
Rhythm: None

Music by
John Williams

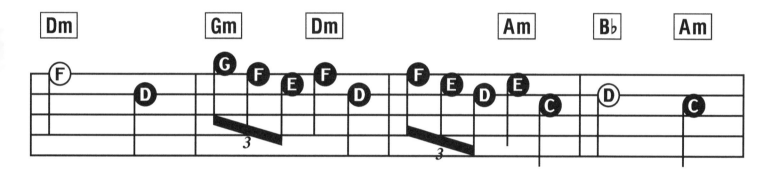

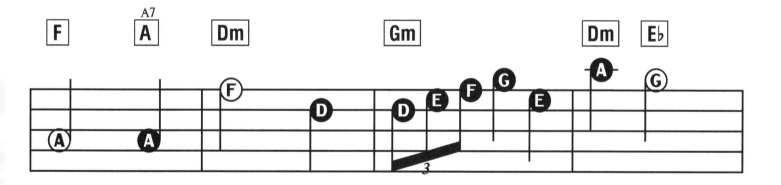

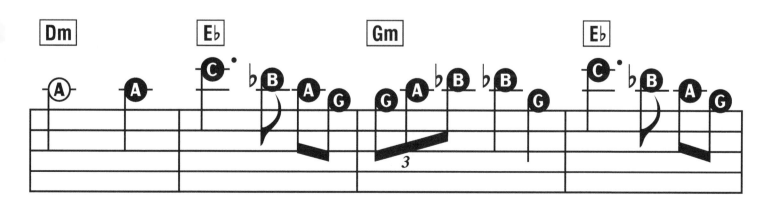

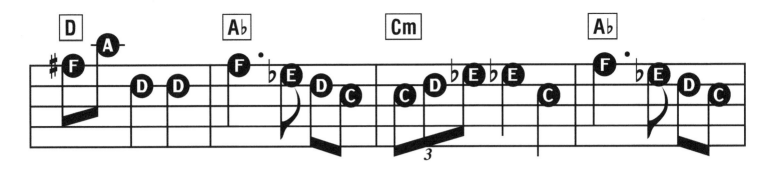

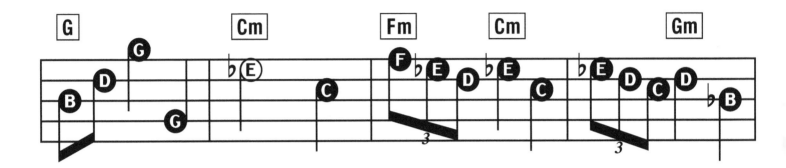

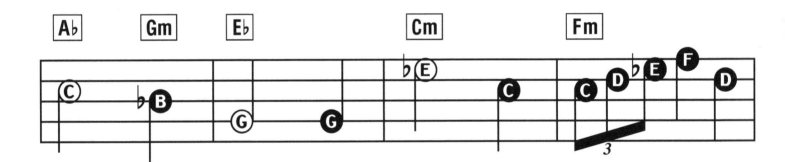

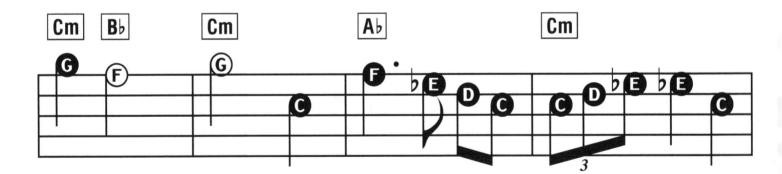

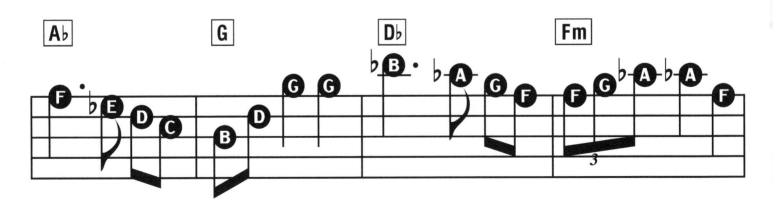

5

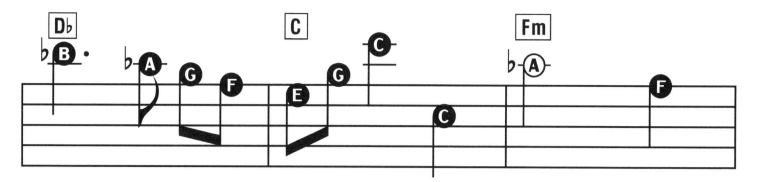

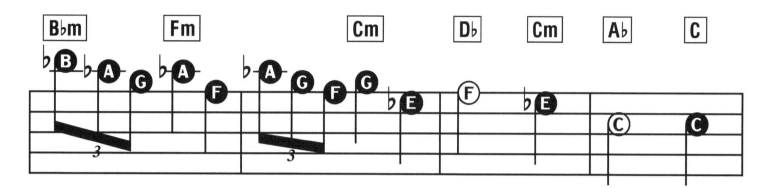

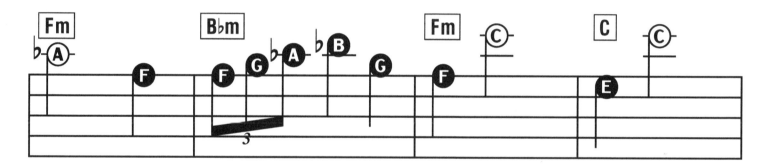

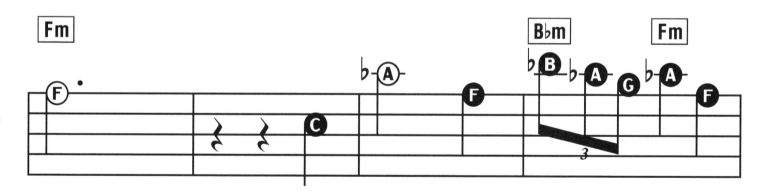

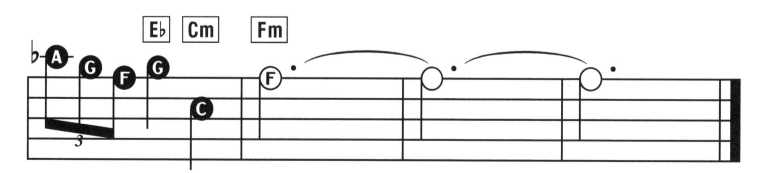

Born on the Fourth of July

from BORN ON THE FOURTH OF JULY

Registration 3
Rhythm: None

Music by
John Williams

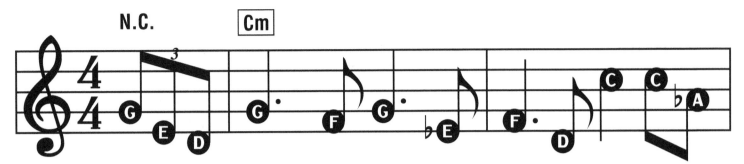

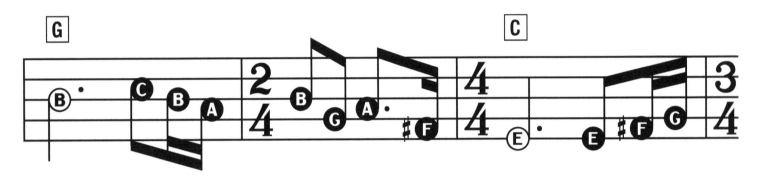

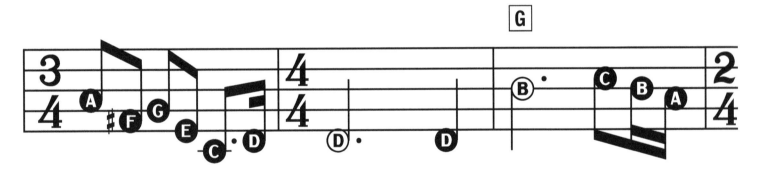

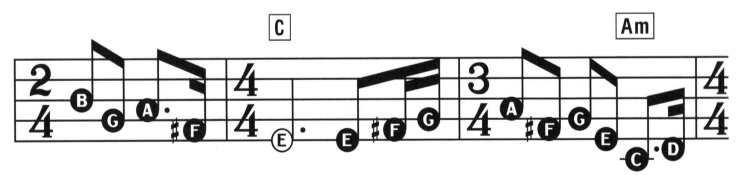

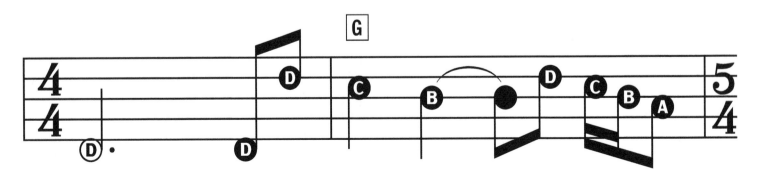

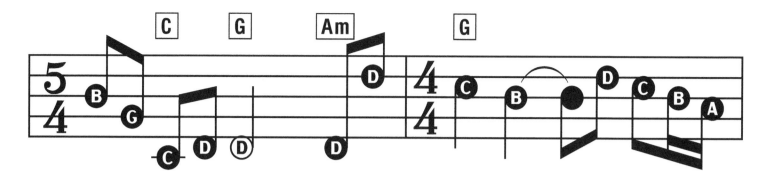

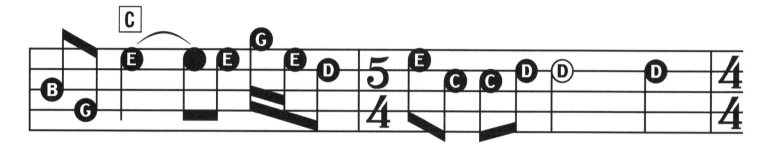

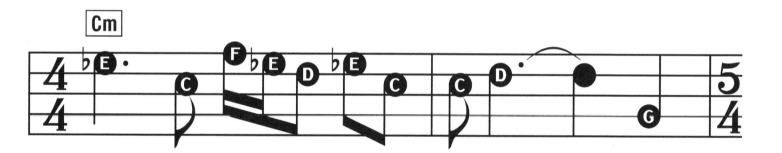

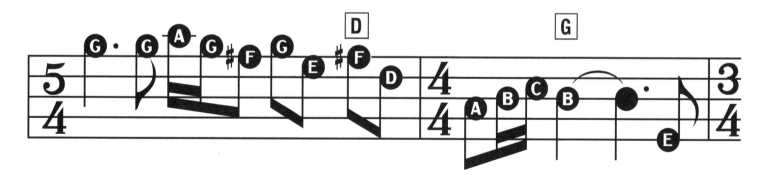

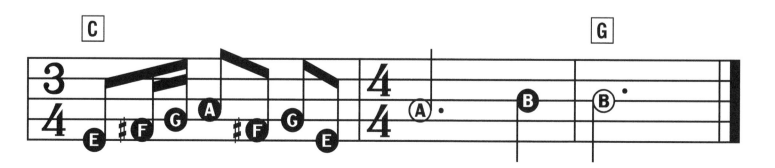

Cantina Band

from STAR WARS: EPISODE IV – A NEW HOPE

Registration 7
Rhythm: Dixieland or Swing

Music by
John Williams

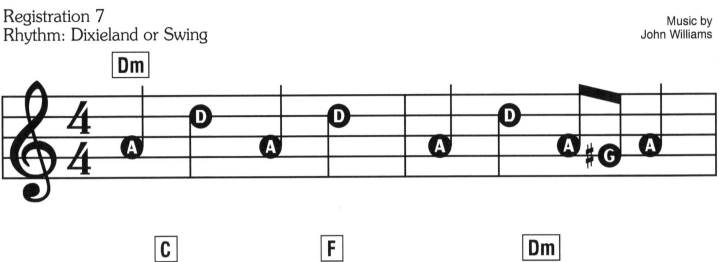

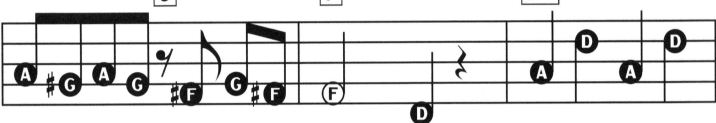

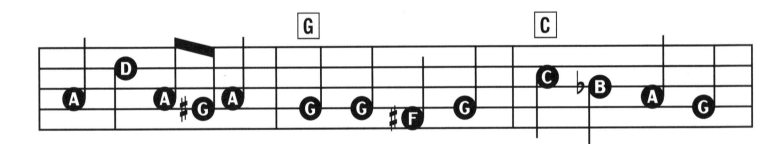

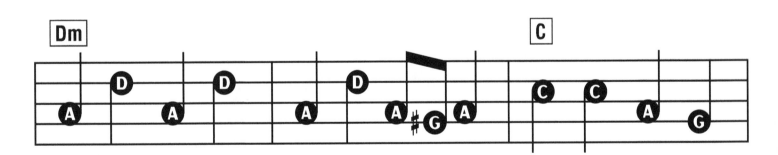

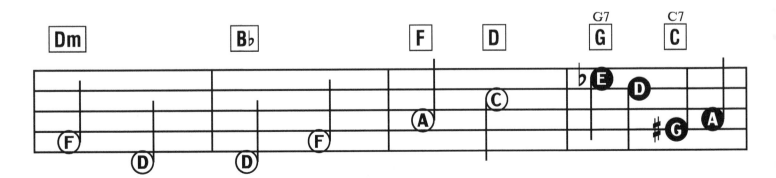

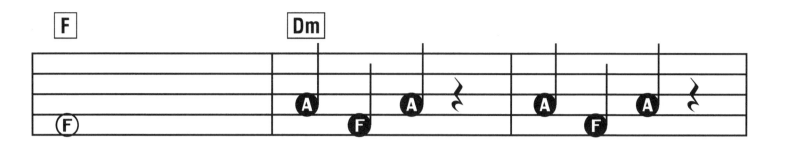

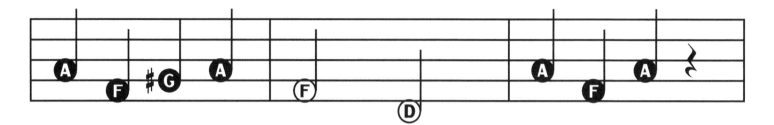

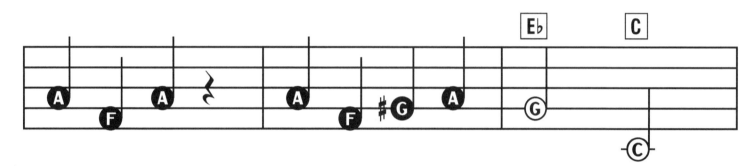

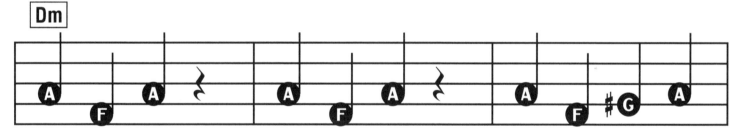

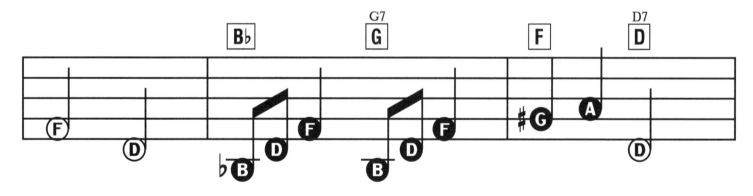

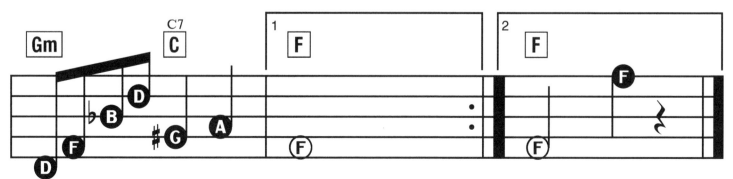

Theme from E.T.
(The Extra-Terrestrial)
from the Universal Picture E.T. (THE EXTRA-TERRESTRIAL)

Registration 8
Rhythm: Waltz

Music by
John Williams

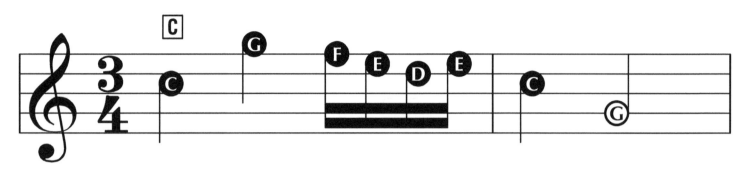

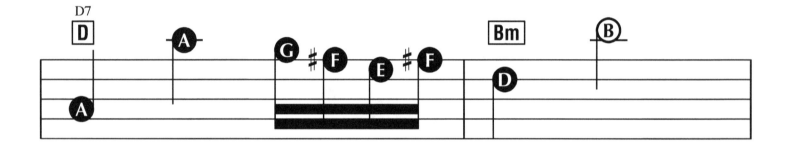

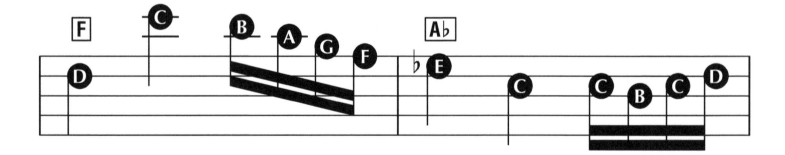

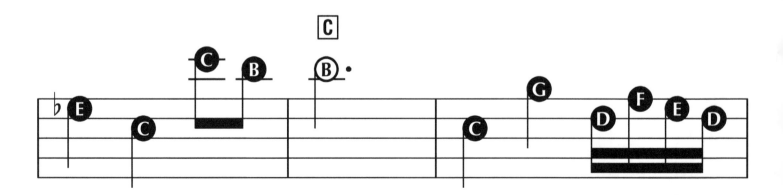

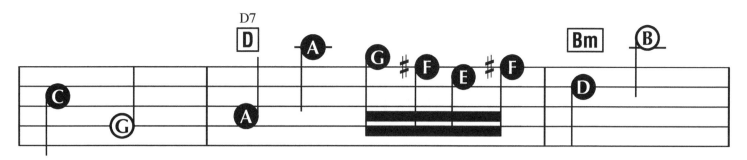

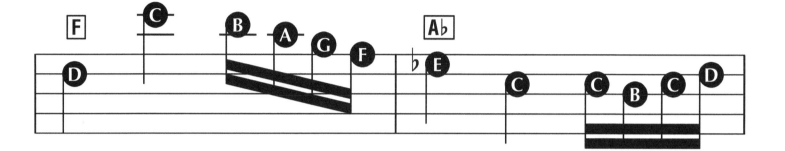

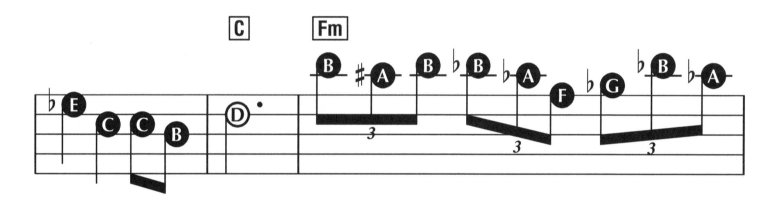

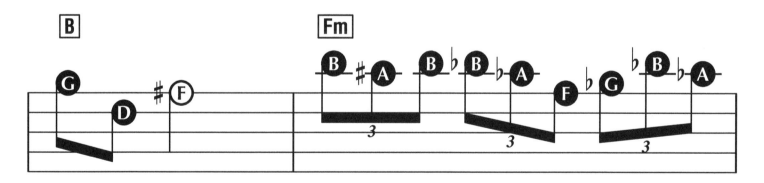

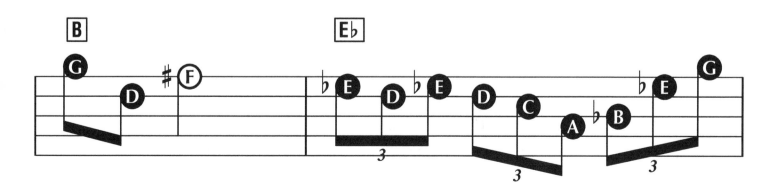

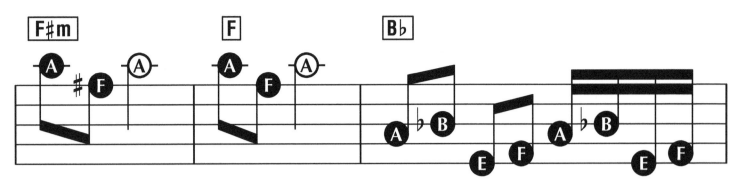

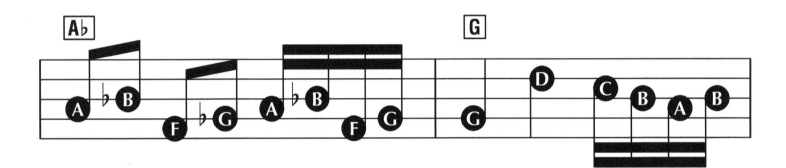

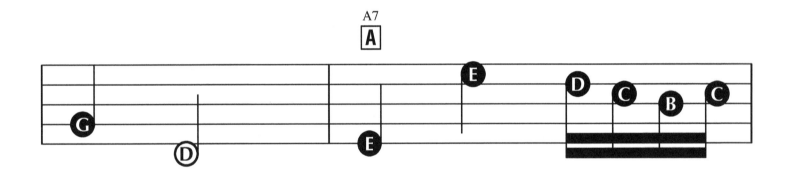

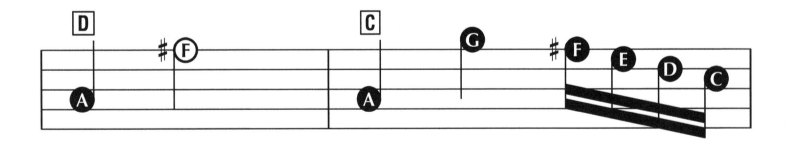

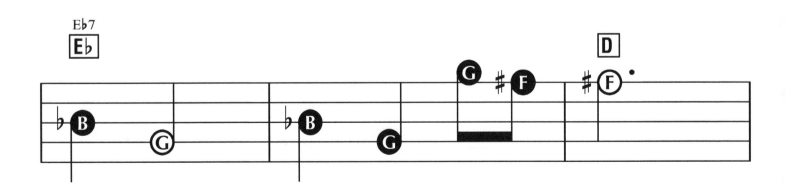

13

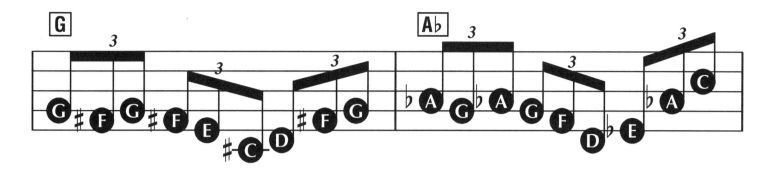

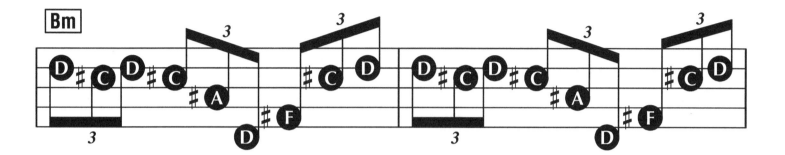

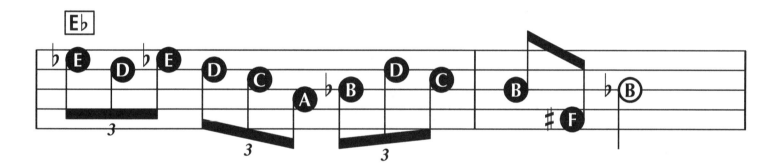

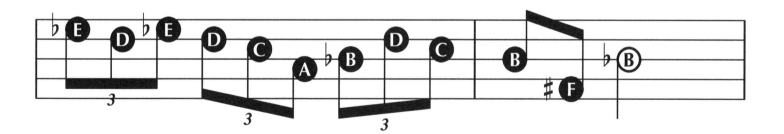

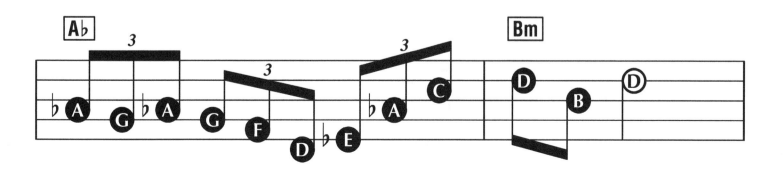

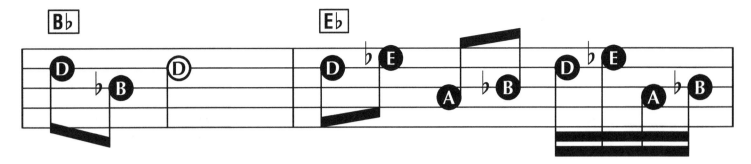

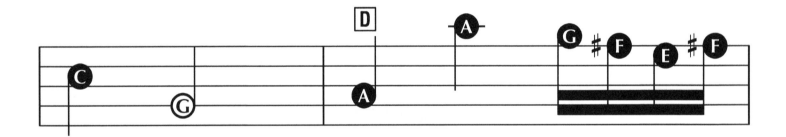

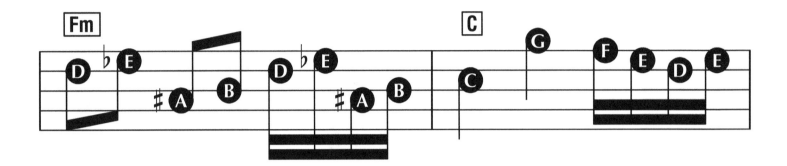

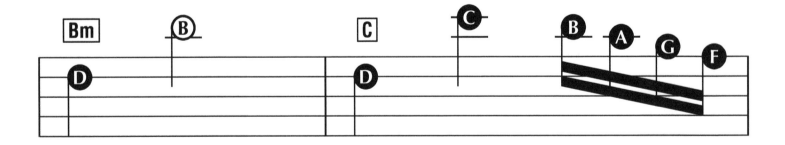

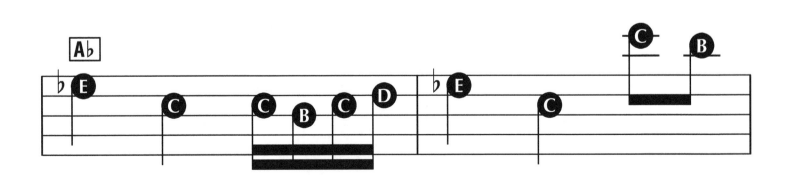

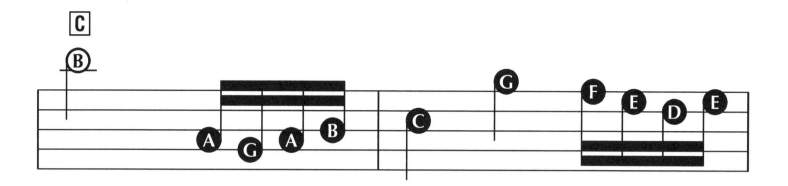

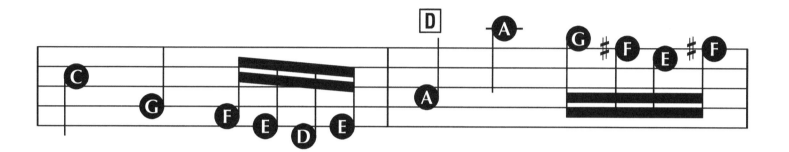

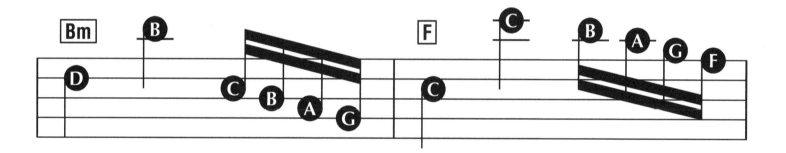

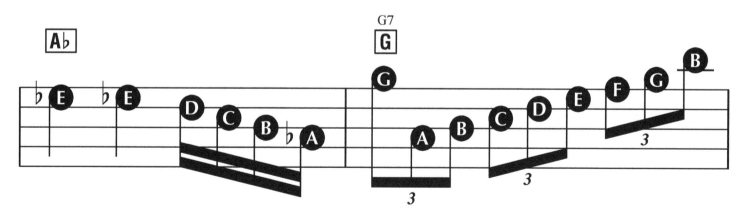

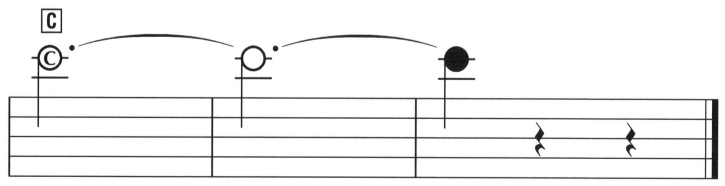

Hedwig's Theme
from the Motion Picture HARRY POTTER AND THE SORCERER'S STONE

Registration 8
Rhythm: Waltz

Music by
John Williams

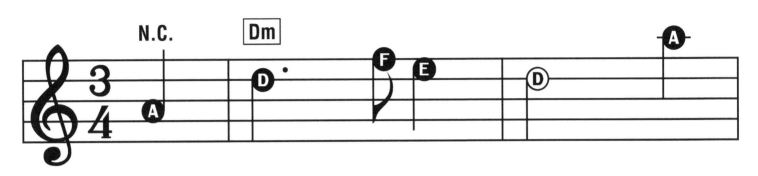

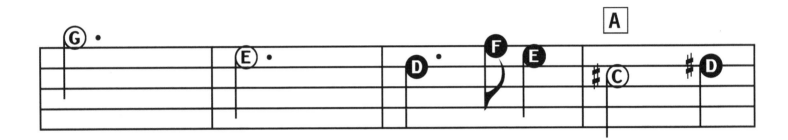

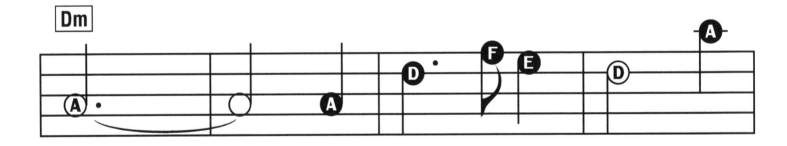

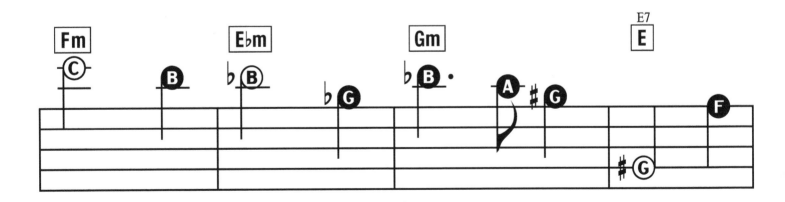

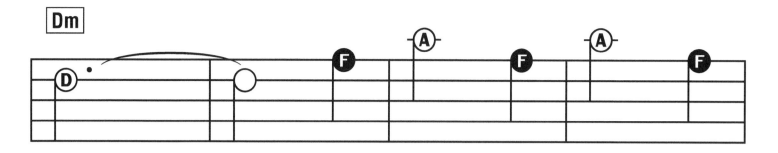

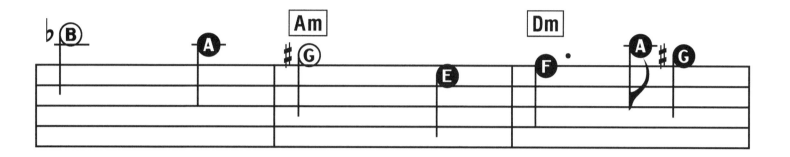

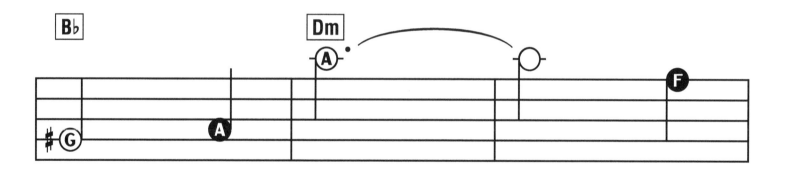

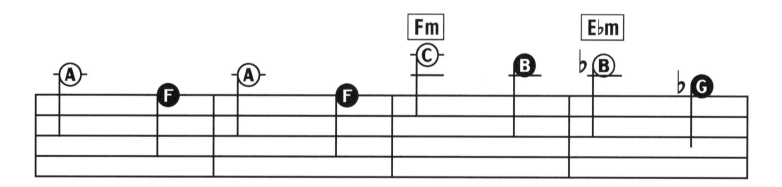

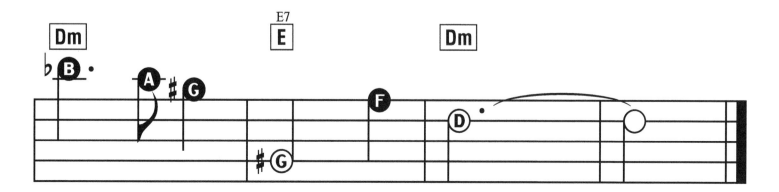

Theme from "Jurassic Park"
from the Universal Motion Picture JURASSIC PARK

Registration 8
Rhythm: Rock or 8-Beat

Composed by
John Williams

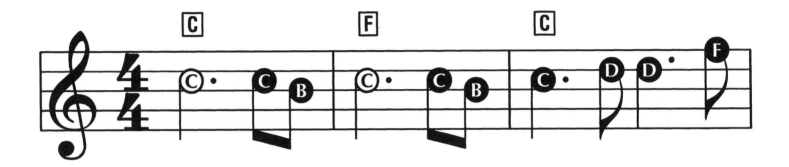

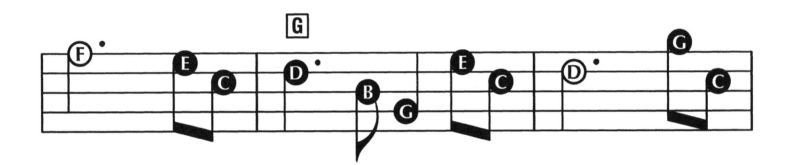

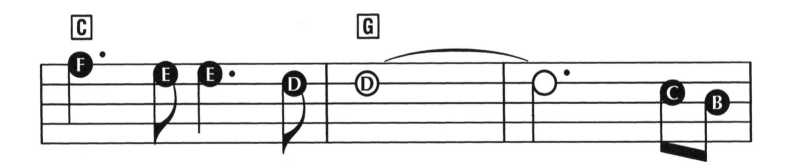

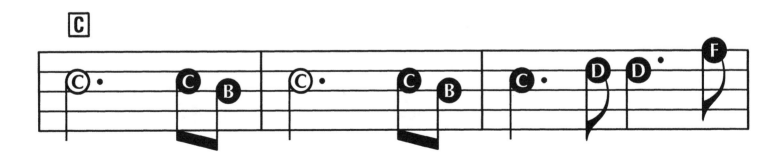

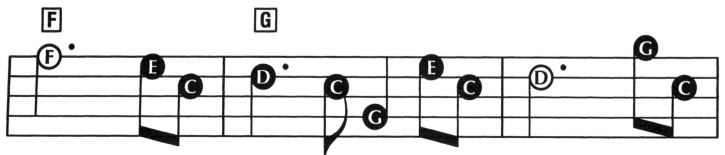

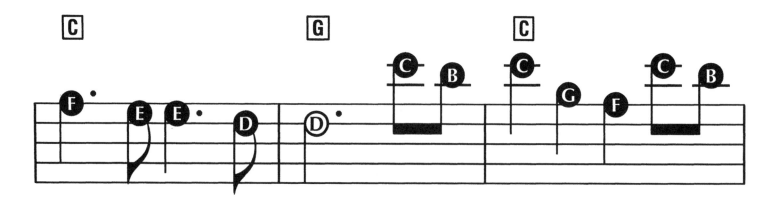

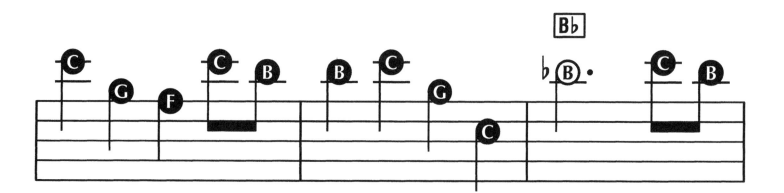

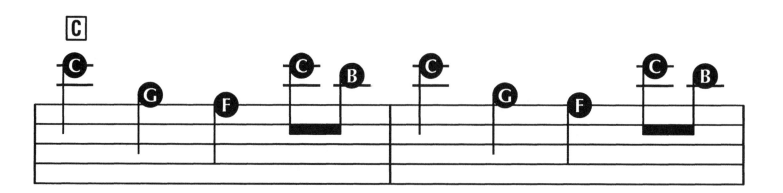

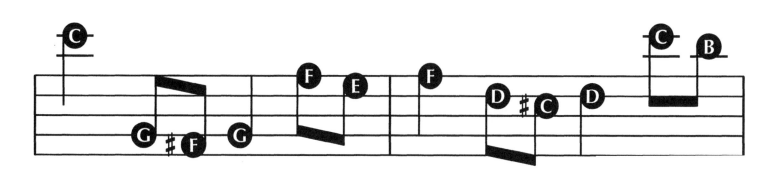

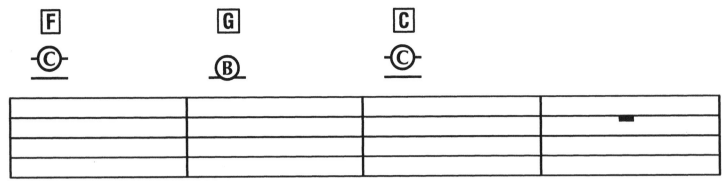

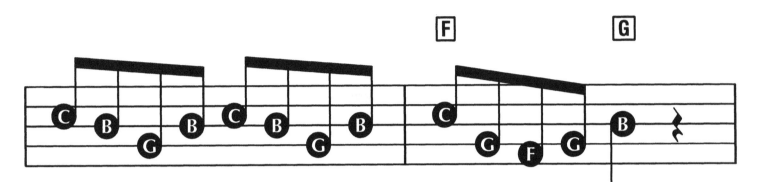

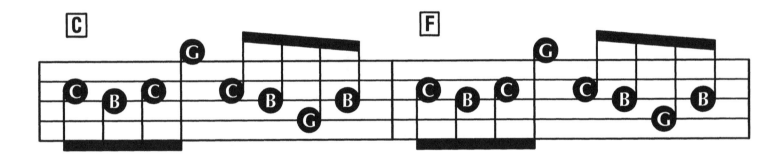

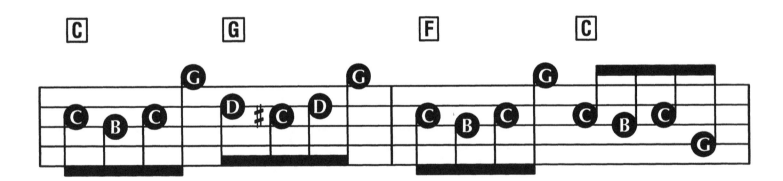

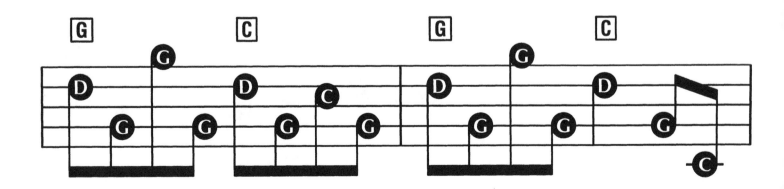

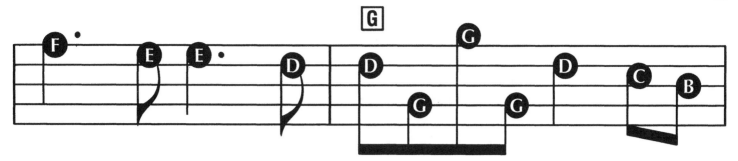

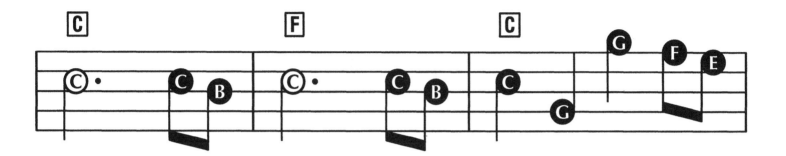

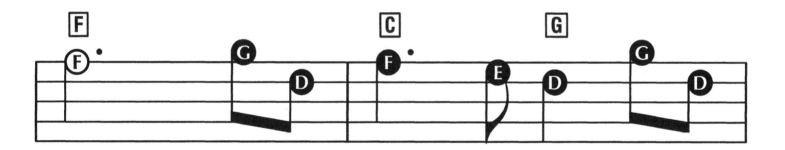

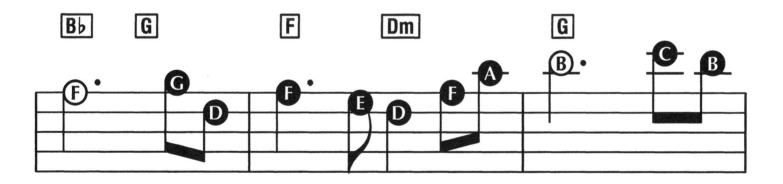

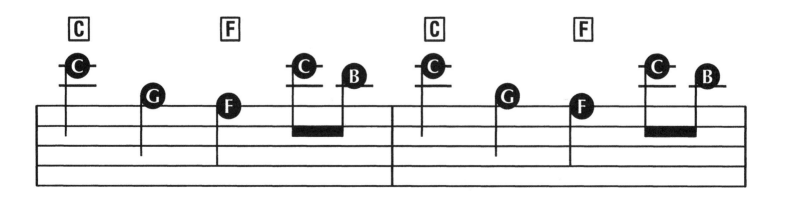

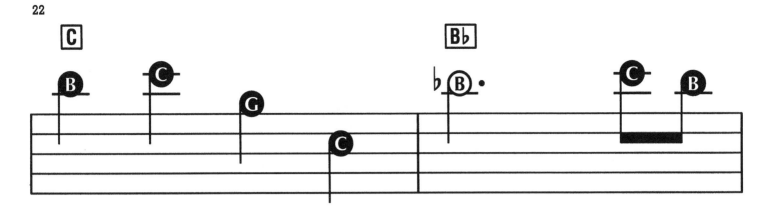

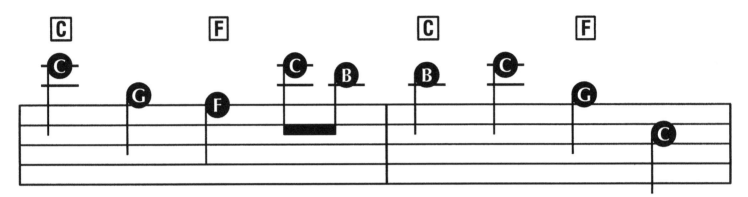

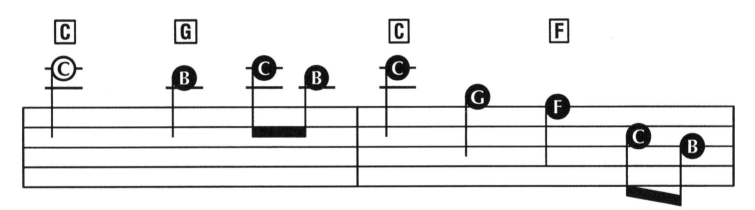

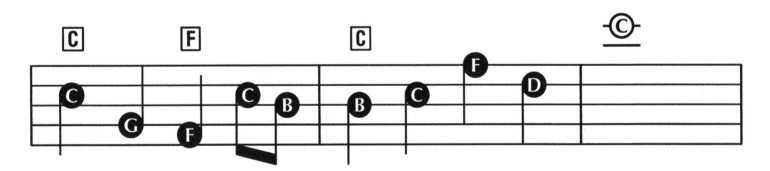

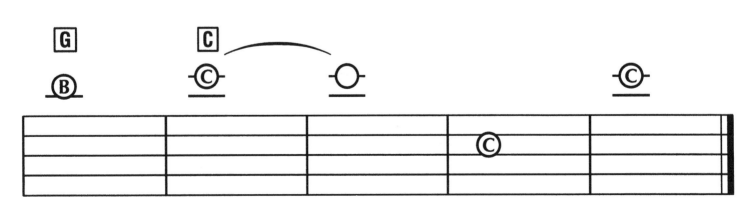

Olympic Fanfare and Theme

Commissioned by the 1984 Los Angeles Olympic Organizing Committee

Registration 2
Rhythm: March

Music by
John Williams

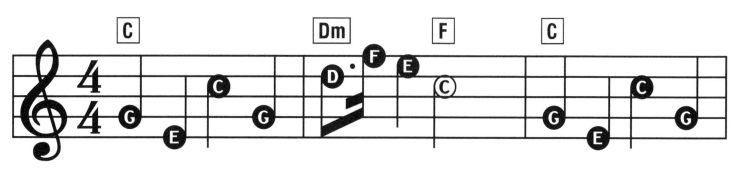

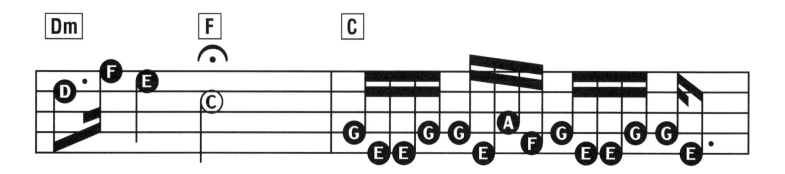

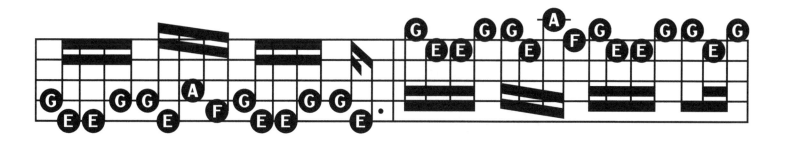

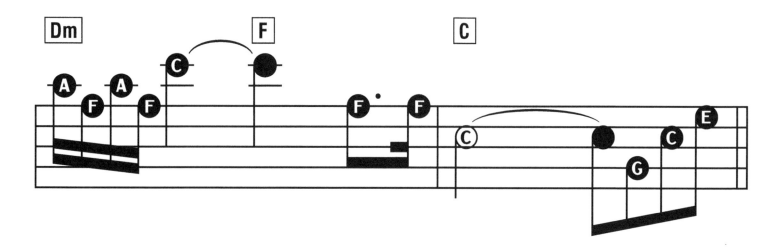

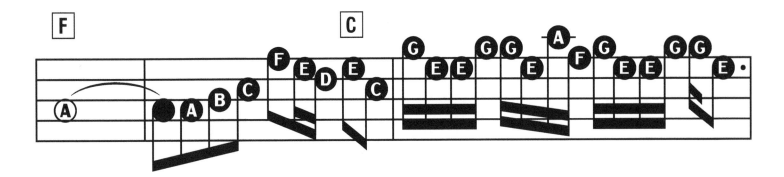

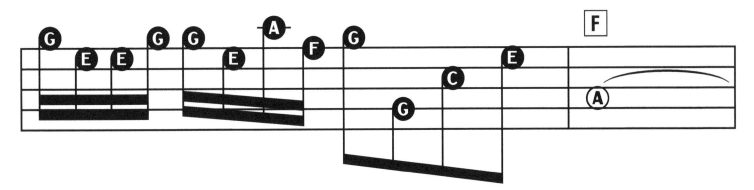

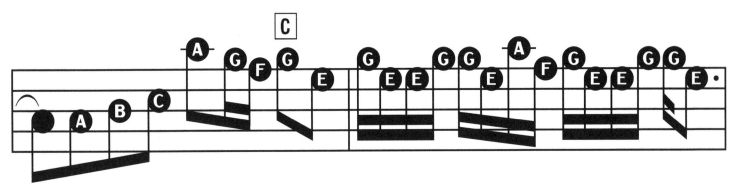

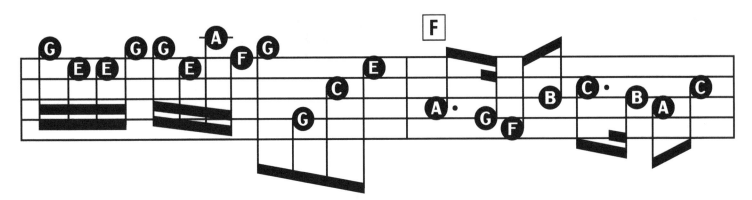

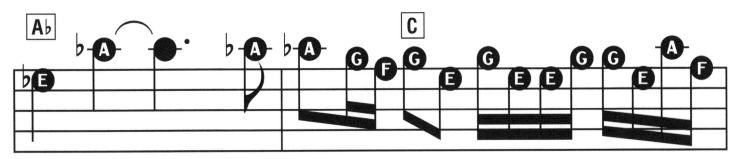

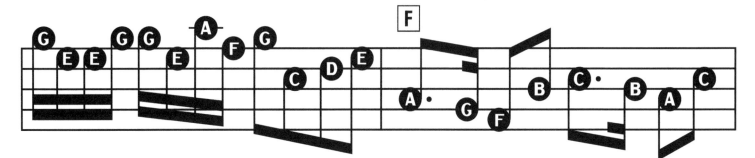

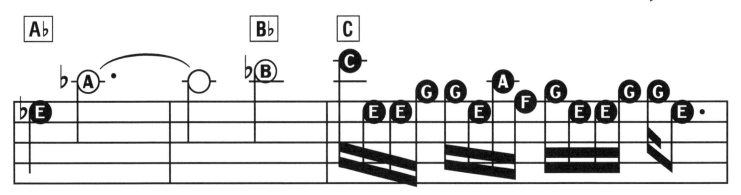

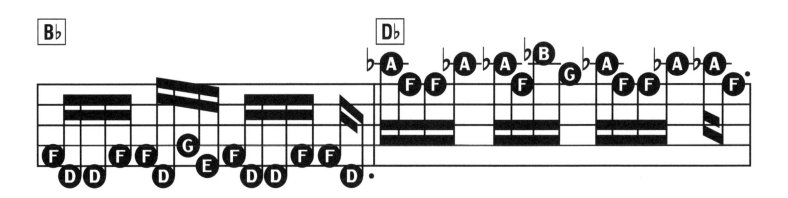

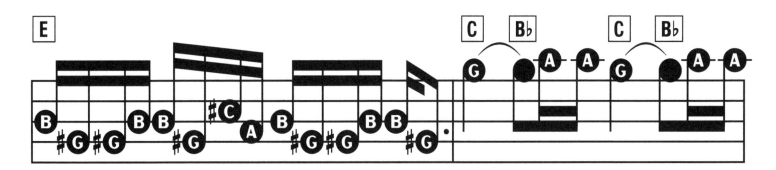

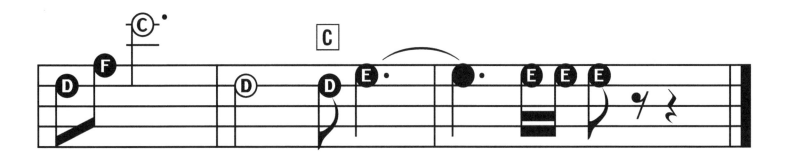

Moonlight
from the Paramount Motion Picture SABRINA

Registration 1
Rhythm: Bossa Nova

Lyric by Alan and Marilyn Bergman
Music by John Williams

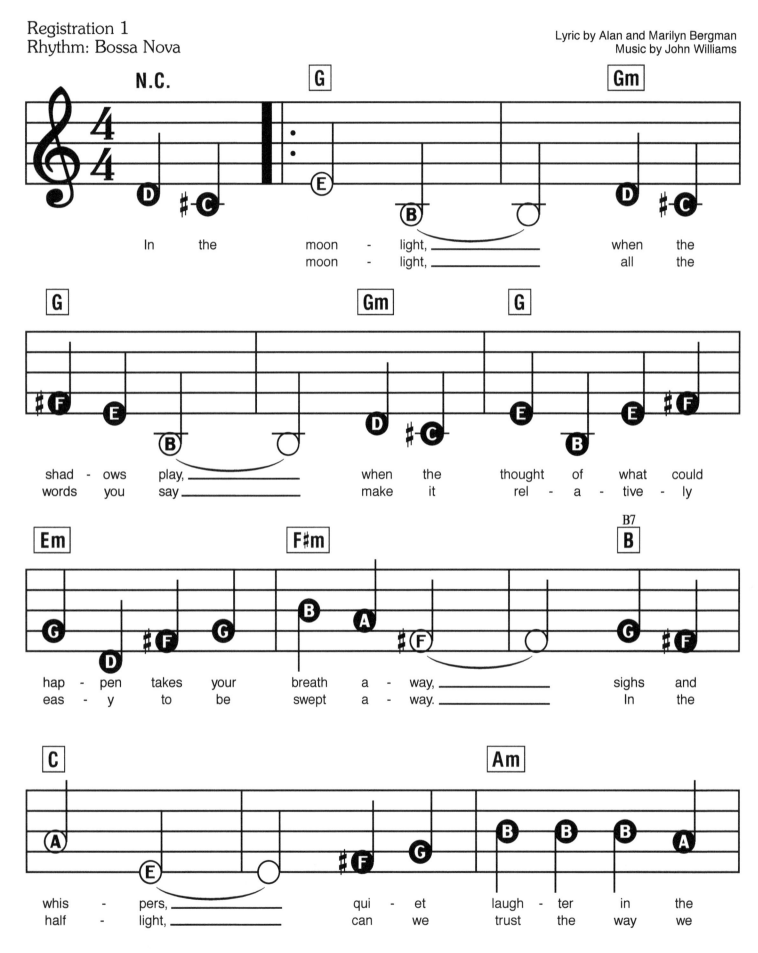

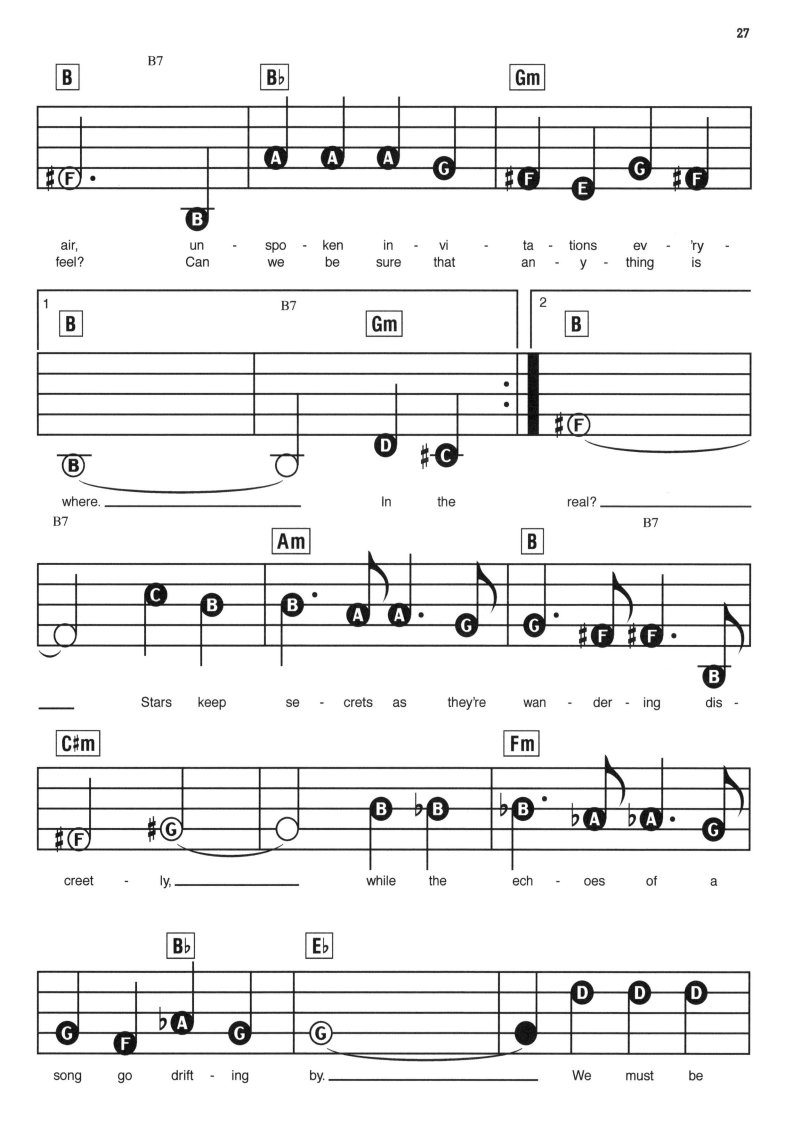

air,   un - spo - ken   in - vi -   ta - tions   ev - 'ry -
feel?   Can   we   be   sure   that   an - y - thing   is

where. _____   In   the   real? _____

_____   Stars   keep   se - crets   as   they're   wan - der - ing   dis -

creet - ly, _____   while   the   ech - oes   of   a

song   go   drift - ing   by. _____   We   must   be

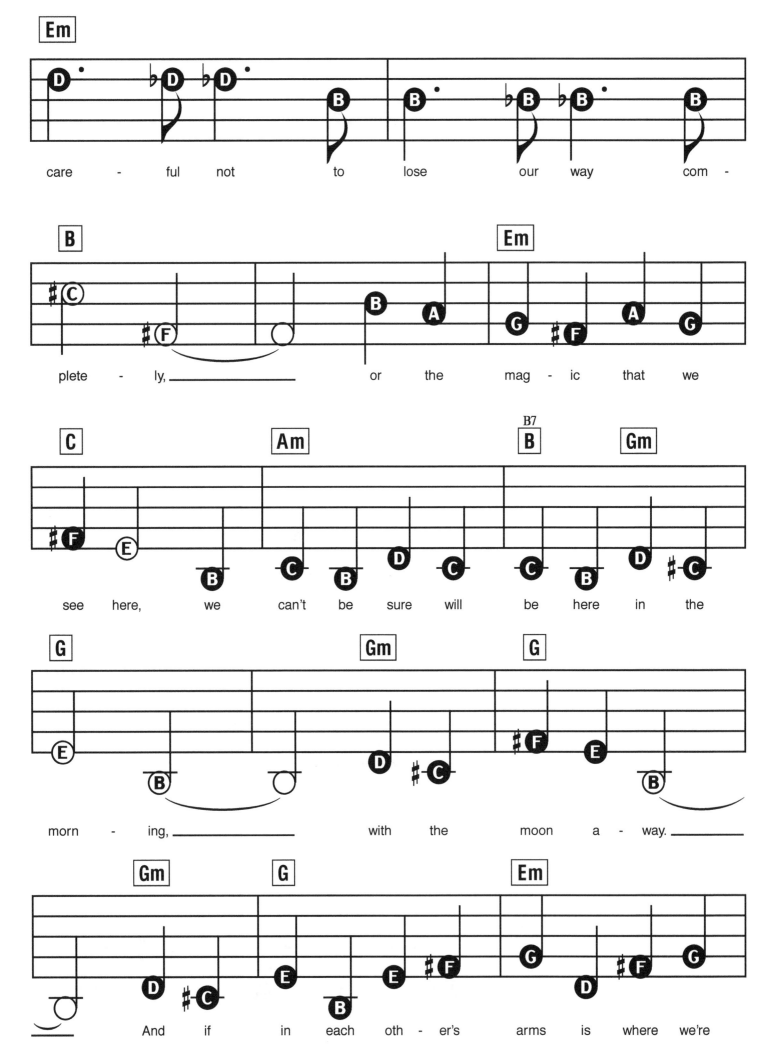

29

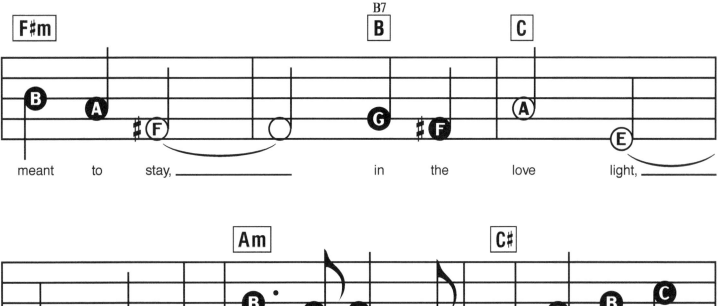

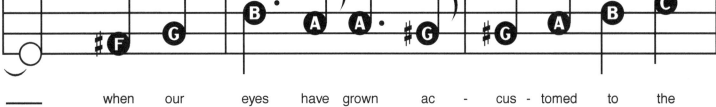

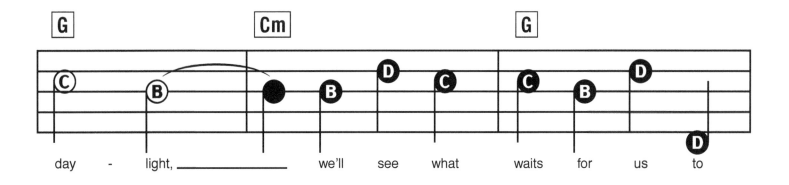

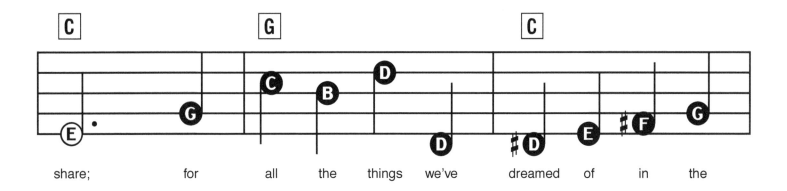

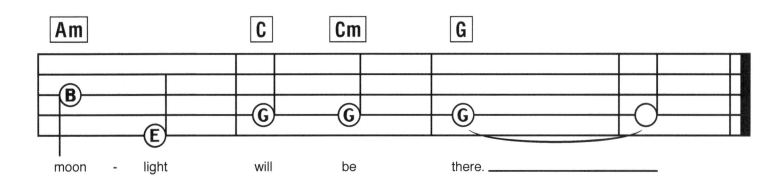

Raiders March
from the Paramount Motion Picture
RAIDERS OF THE LOST ARK

Music by
John Williams

Registration 4
Rhythm: March

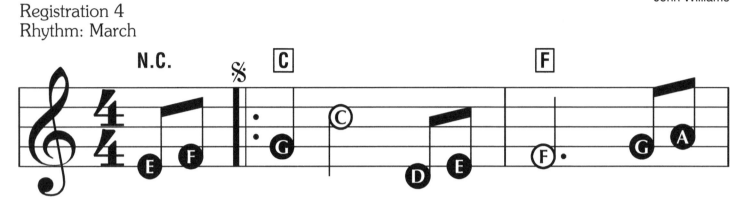

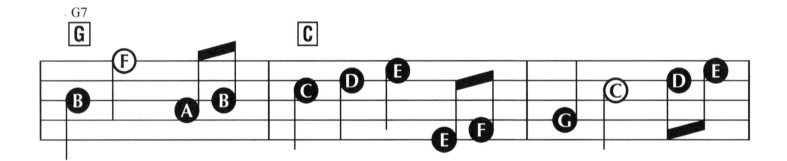

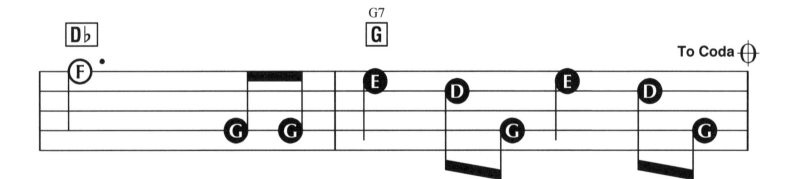

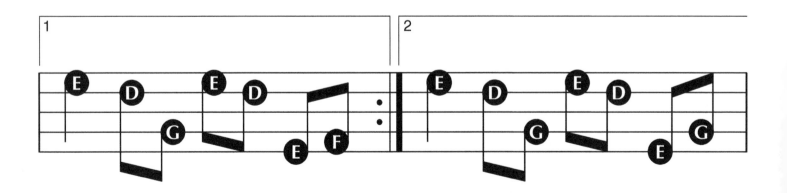

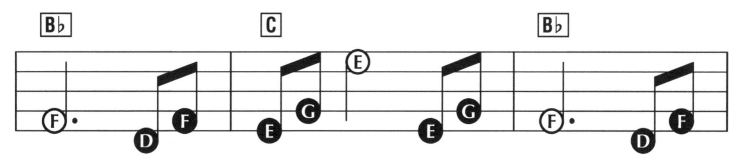

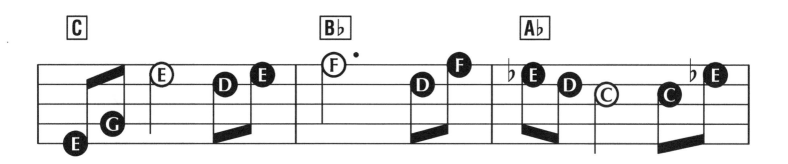

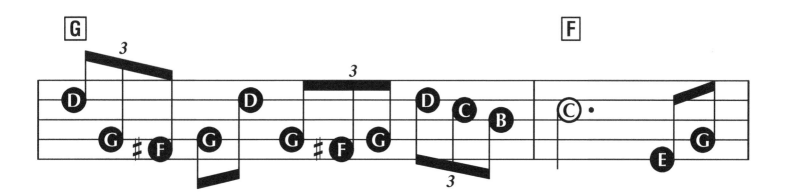

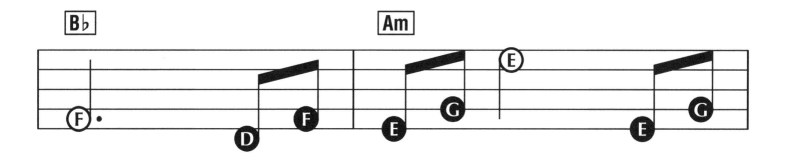

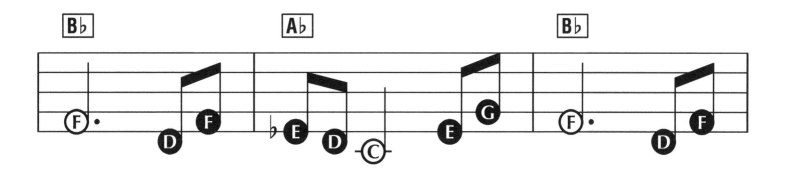

32

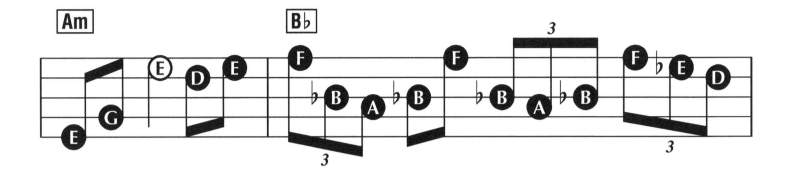

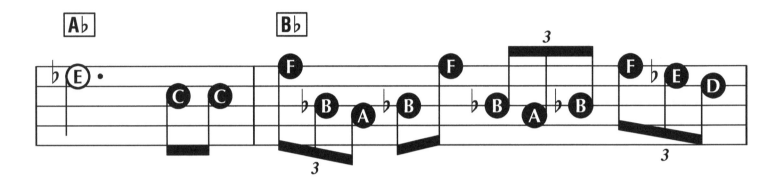

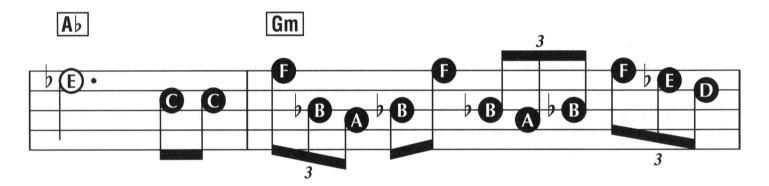

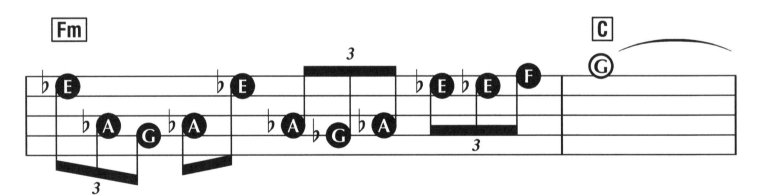

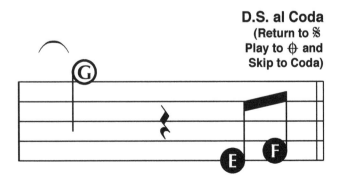

D.S. al Coda
(Return to 𝄋
Play to ⊕ and
Skip to Coda)

CODA
⊕

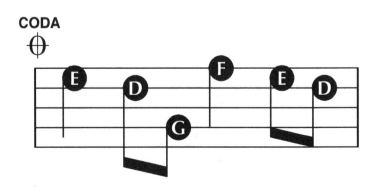

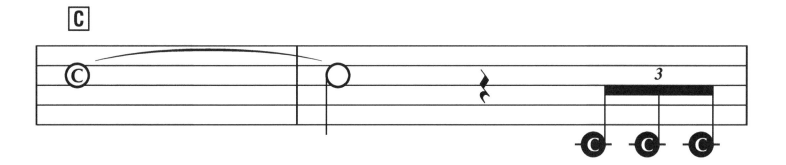

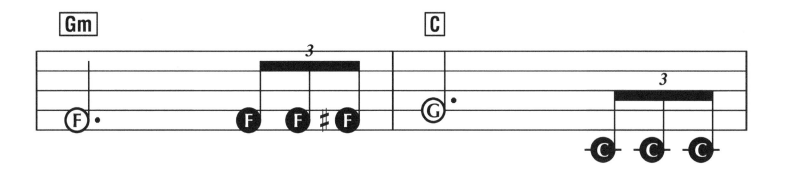

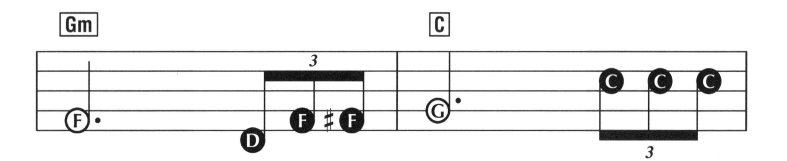

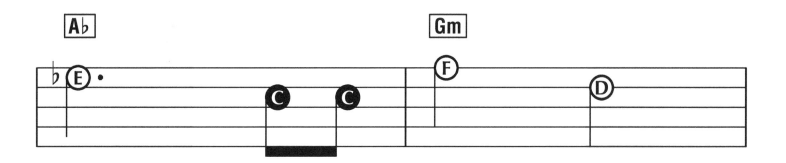

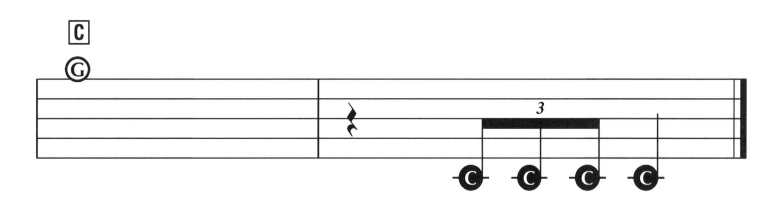

Theme from "Schindler's List"
from the Universal Motion Picture SCHINDLER'S LIST

Registration 3
Rhythm: Ballad

Music by
John Williams

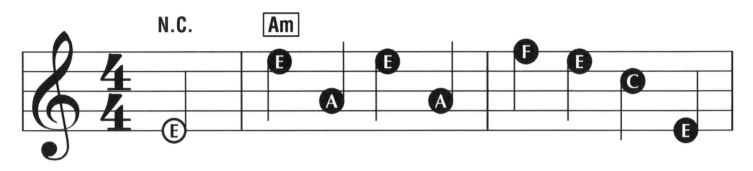

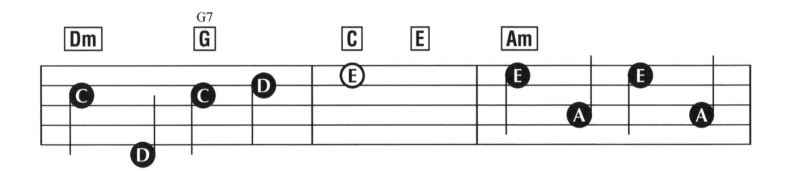

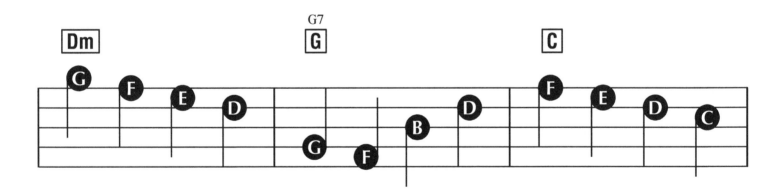

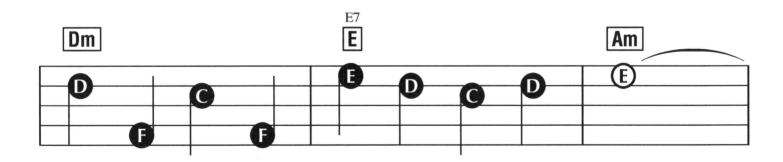

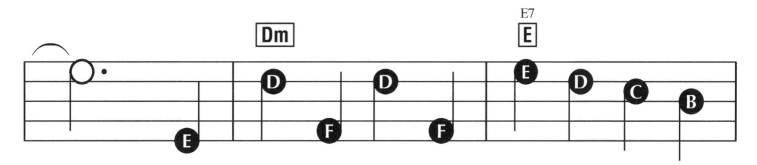

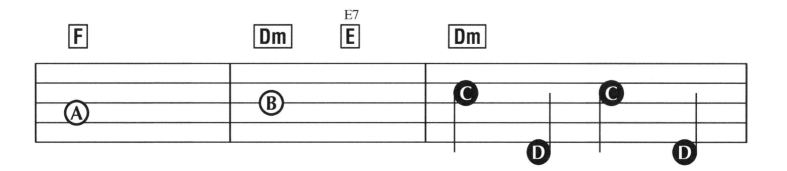

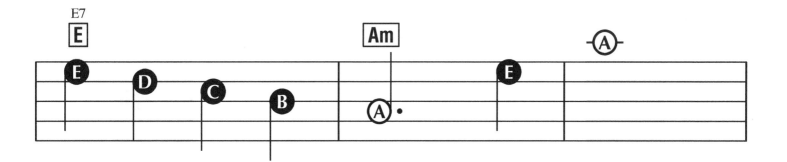

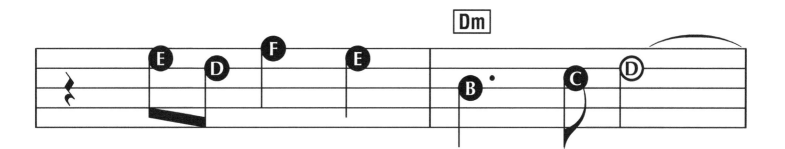

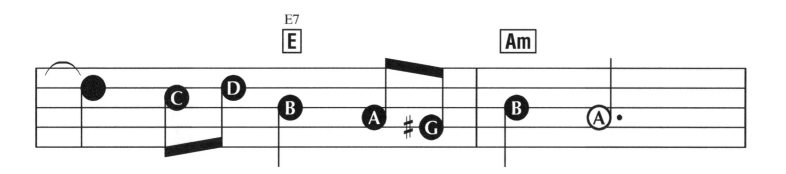

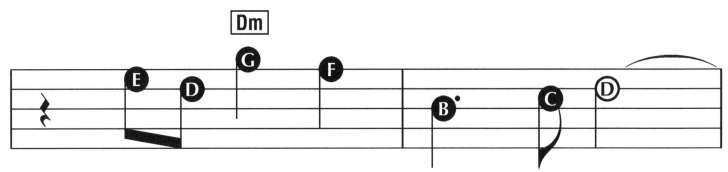

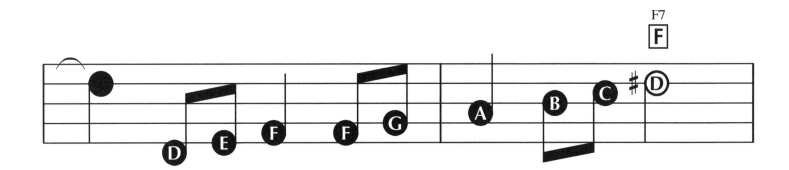

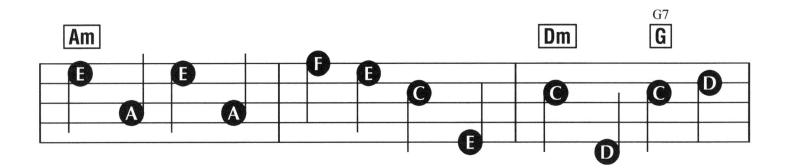

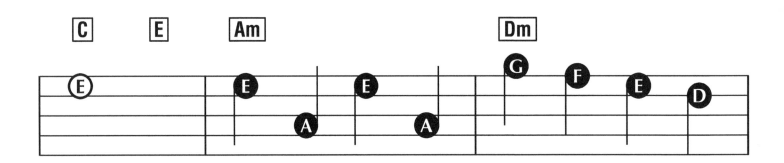

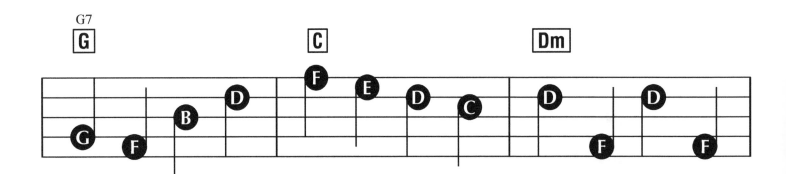

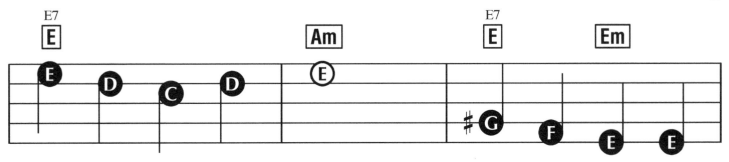

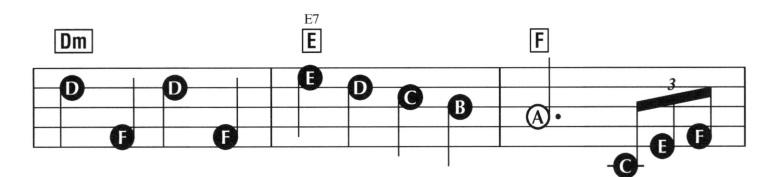

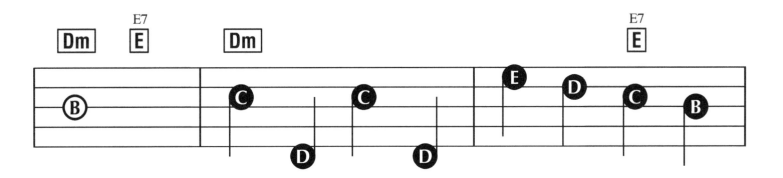

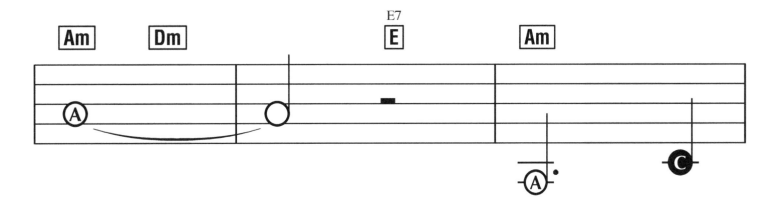

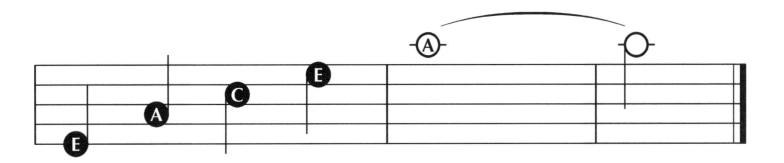

Somewhere in My Memory

from the Twentieth Century Fox Motion Picture HOME ALONE

Registration 3
Rhythm: Ballad

Words by Leslie Bricusse
Music by John Williams

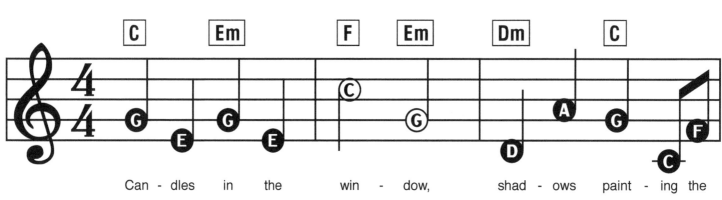

Can - dles in the win - dow, shad - ows paint - ing the

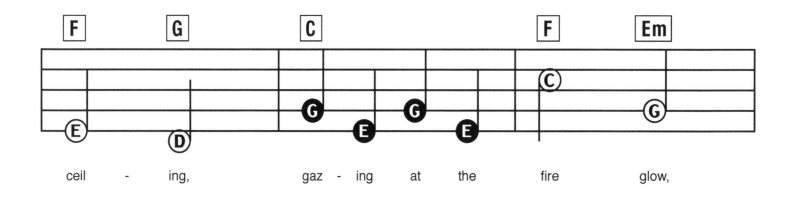

ceil - ing, gaz - ing at the fire glow,

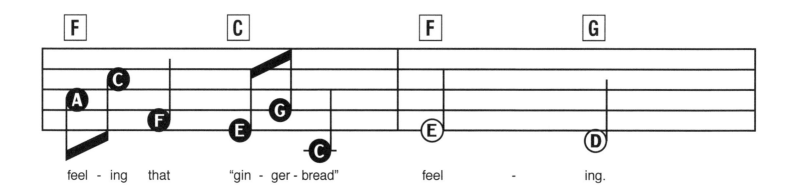

feel - ing that "gin - ger - bread" feel - ing.

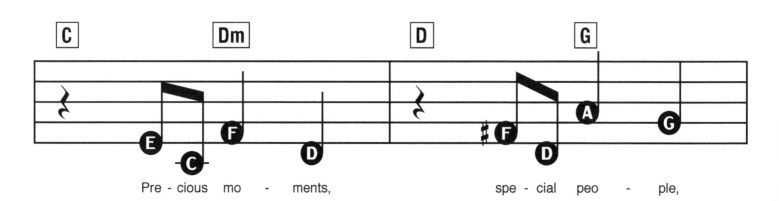

Pre - cious mo - ments, spe - cial peo - ple,

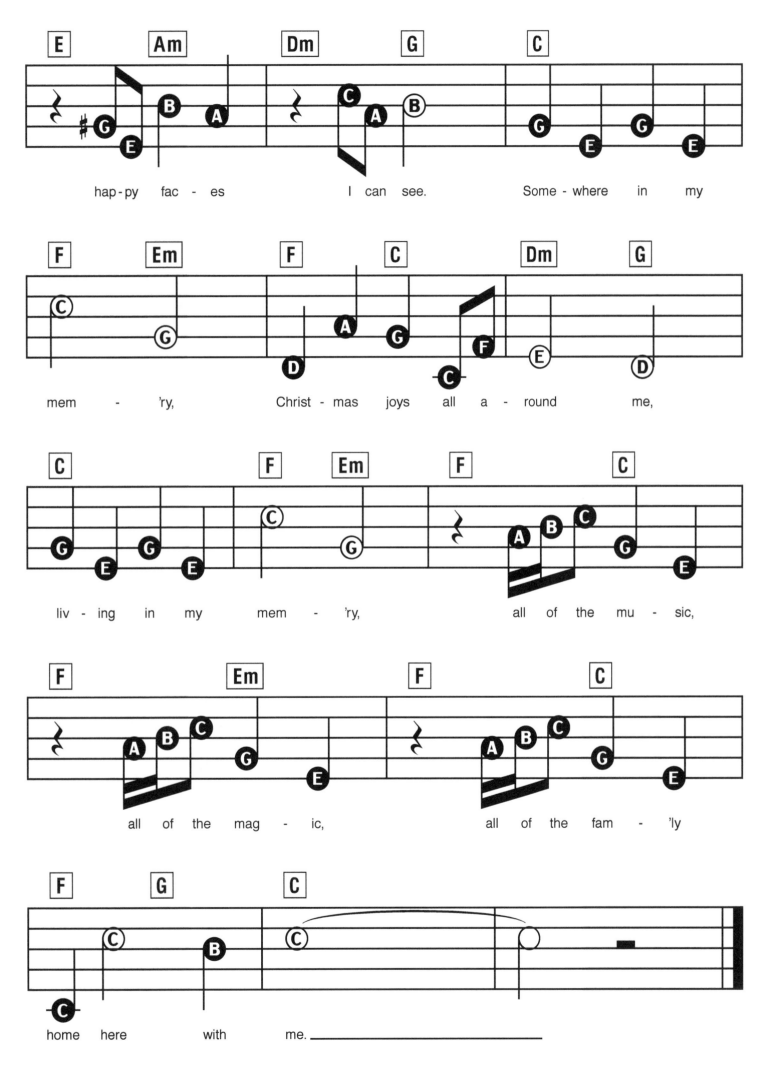

Star Wars
(Main Theme)
from STAR WARS, THE EMPIRE STRIKES BACK
and RETURN OF THE JEDI

Registration 2
Rhythm: March

Music by
John Williams

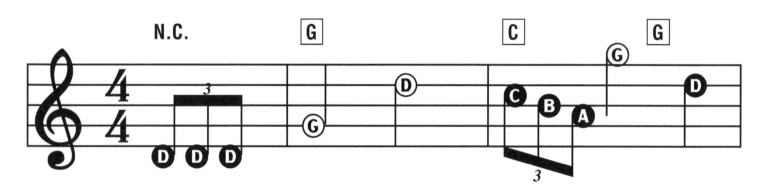

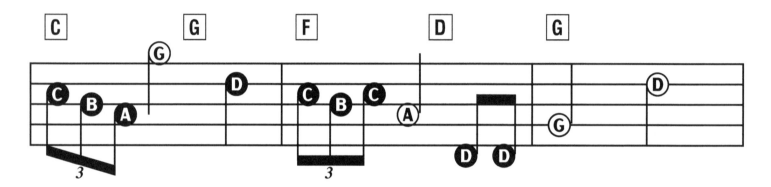

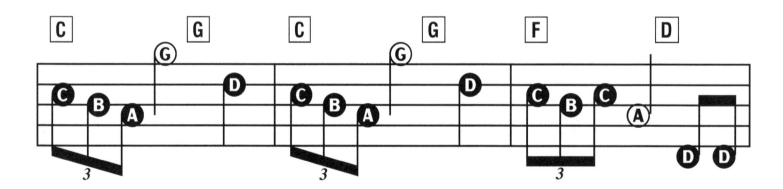

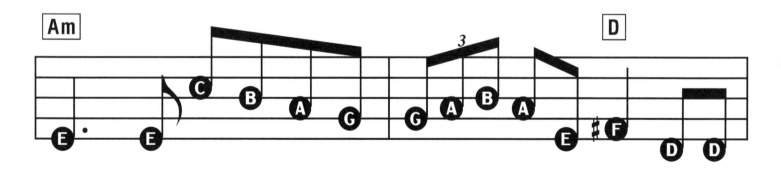

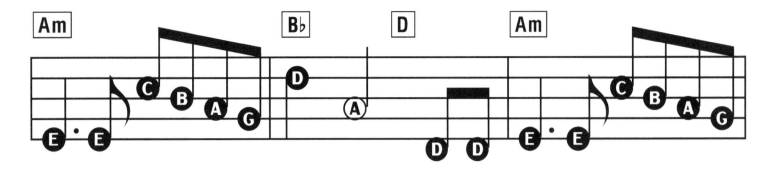

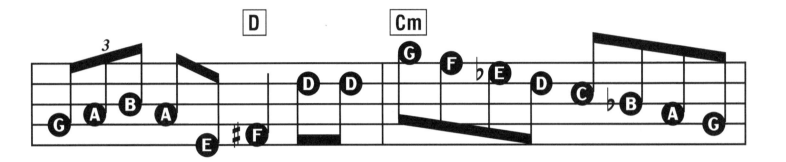

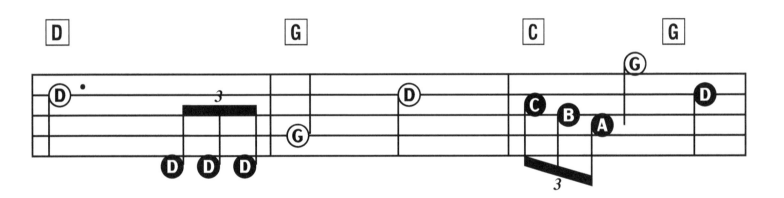

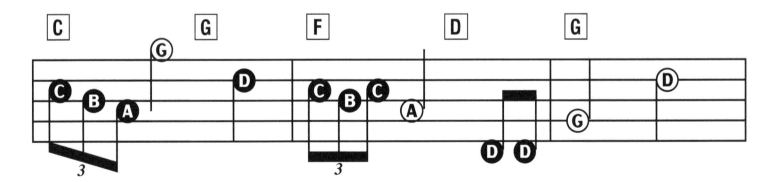

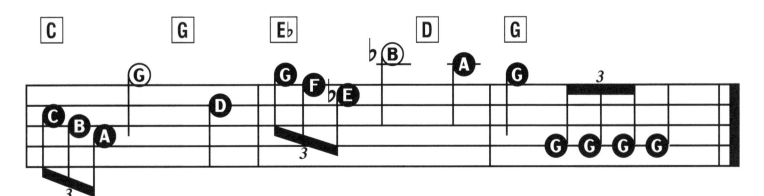

Theme from "Superman"

from SUPERMAN

Registration 7
Rhythm: March

Music by
John Williams

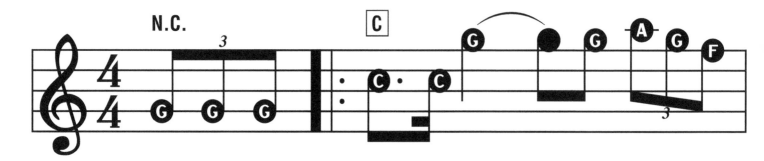

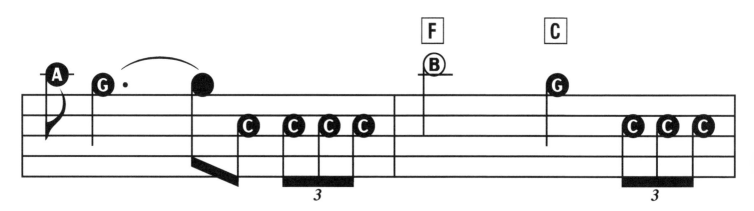

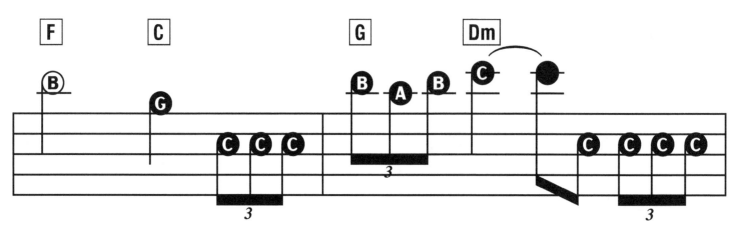

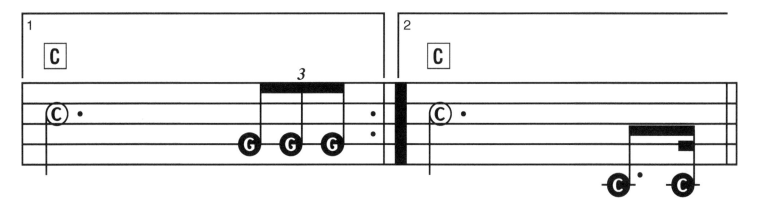

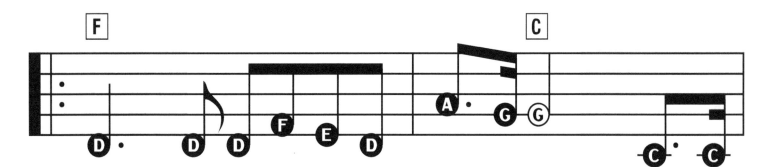

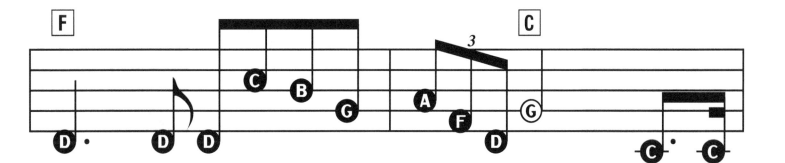

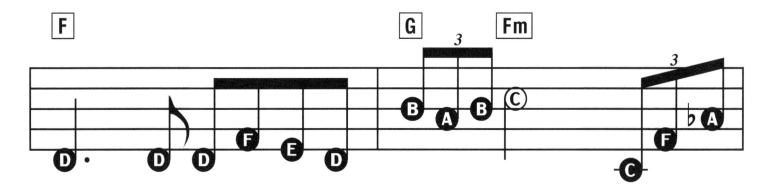

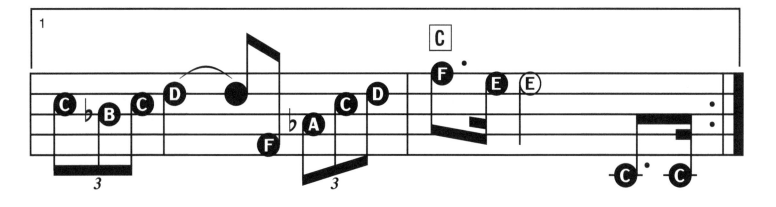

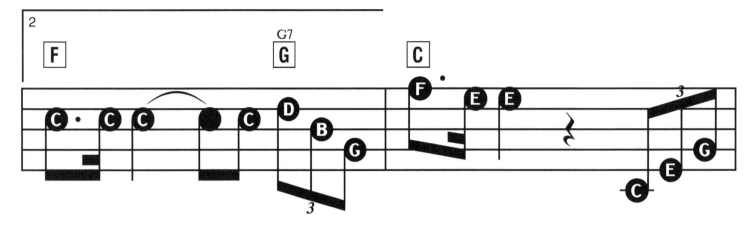

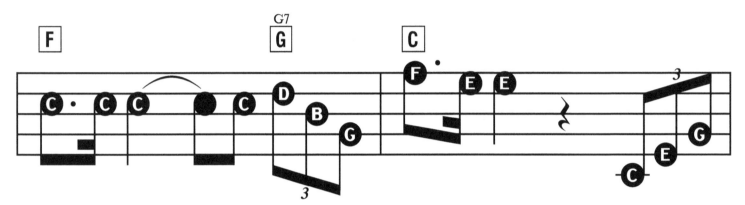

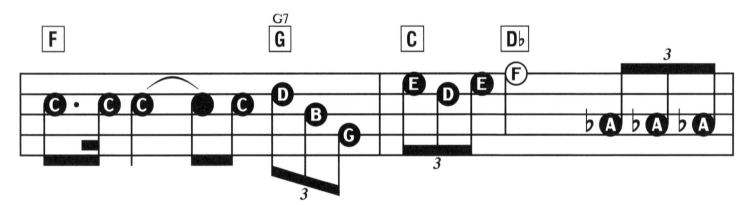

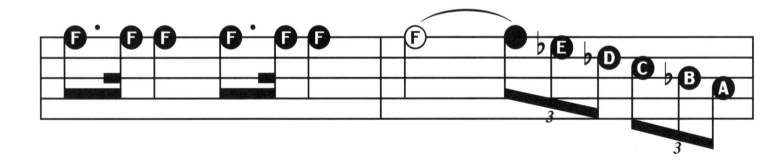

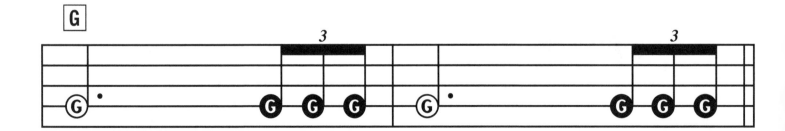

45

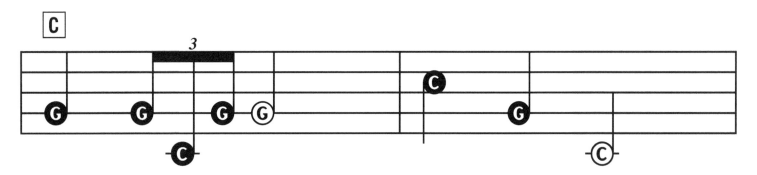

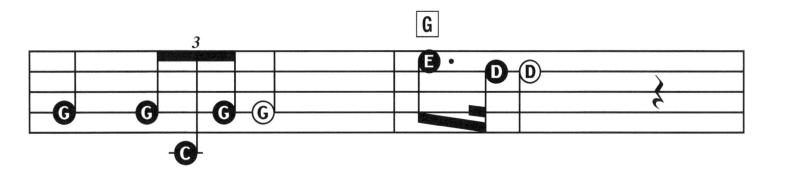

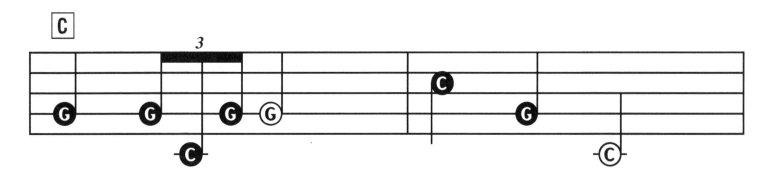

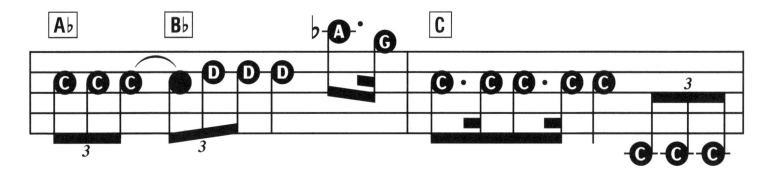

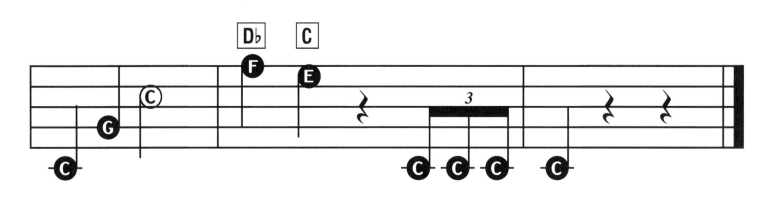

The Throne Room
(and End Title)
from STAR WARS: EPISODE IV – A NEW HOPE

Registration 2
Rhythm: March

Music by
John Williams

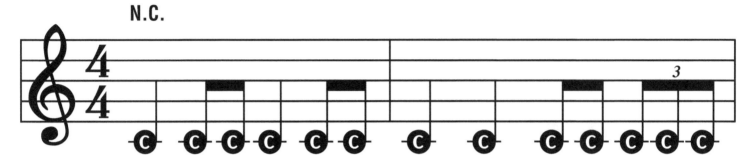

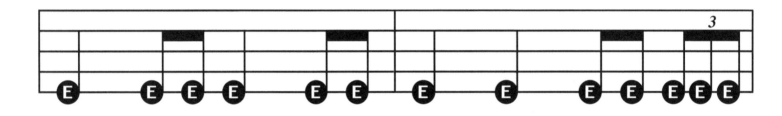

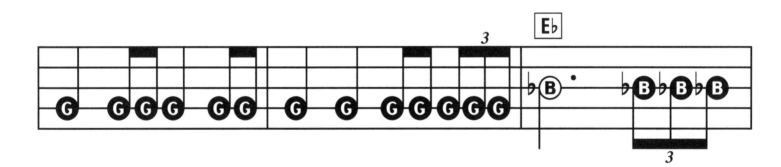

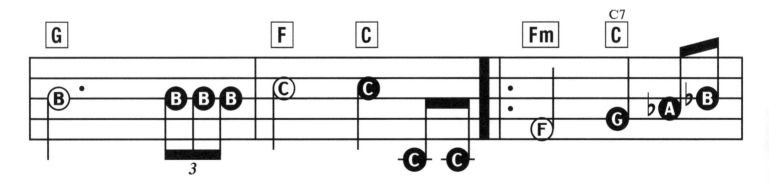

47

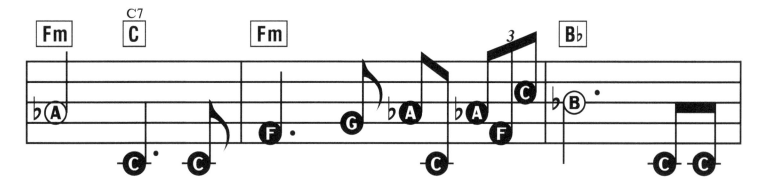

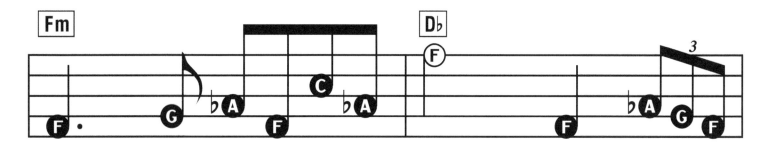

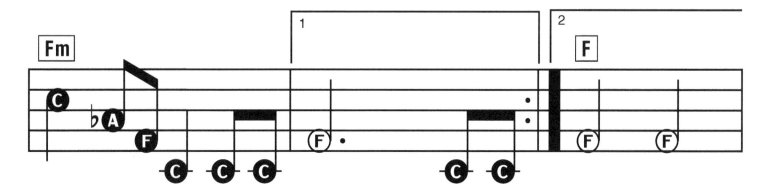

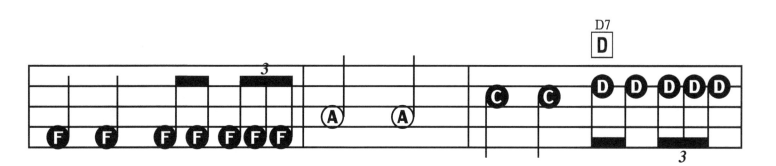

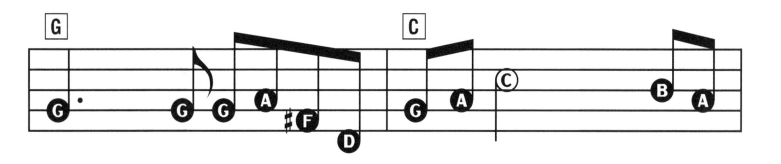

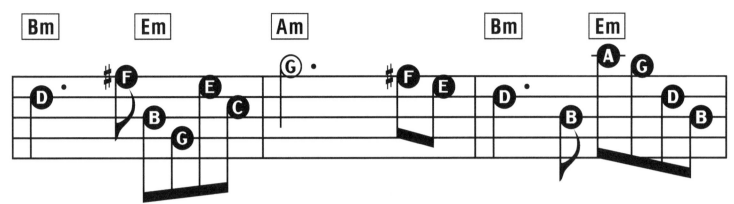

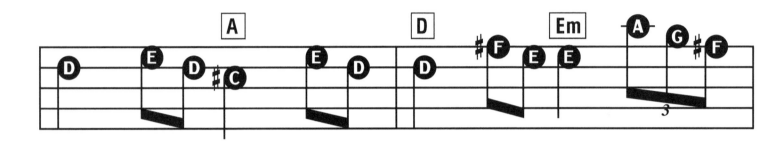

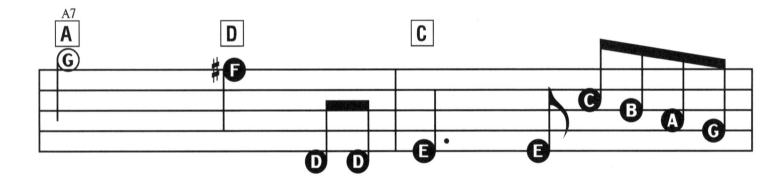

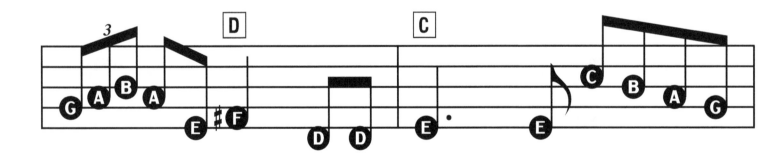

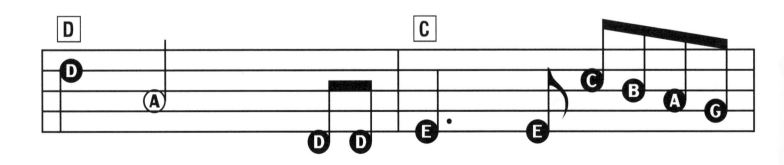

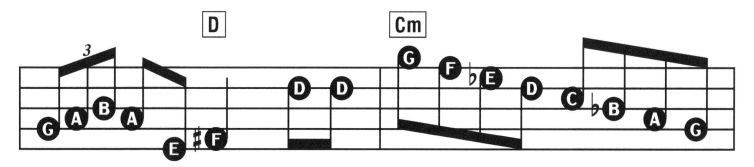

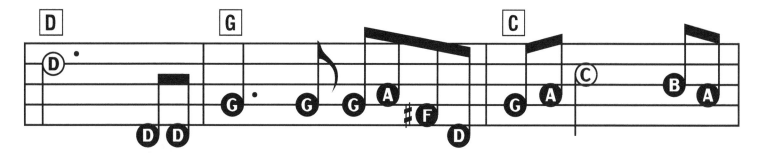

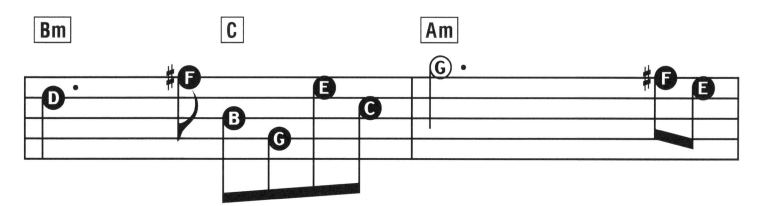

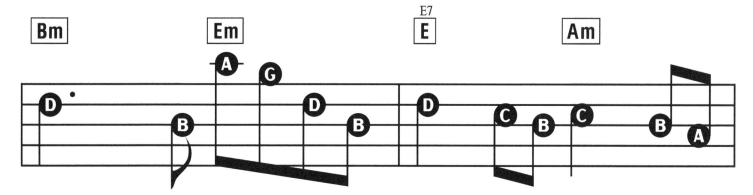

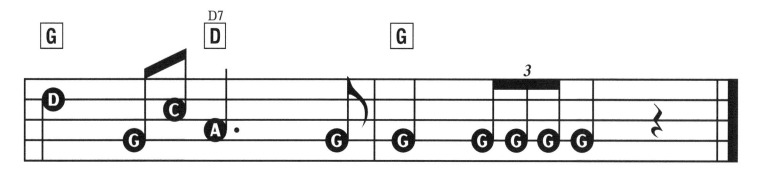

With Malice Toward None
from the Motion Picture LINCOLN

Registration 8
Rhythm: Waltz

Composed by
John Williams

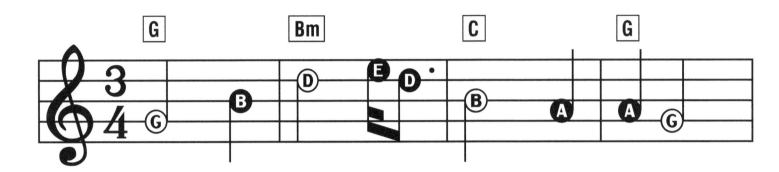

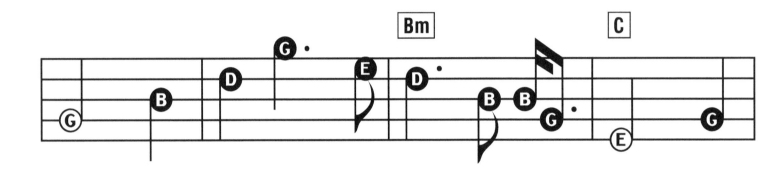

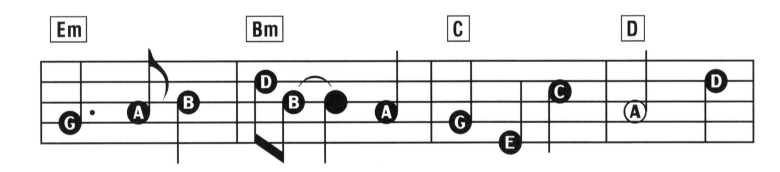

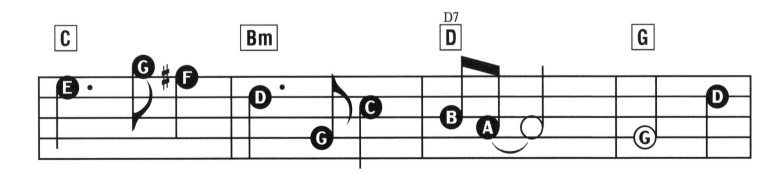

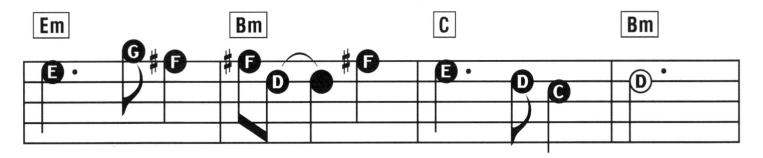

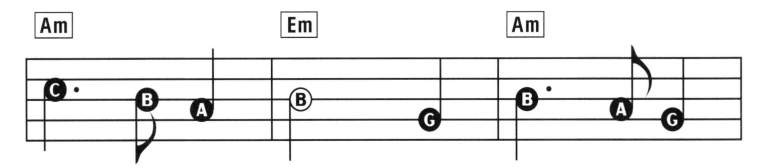

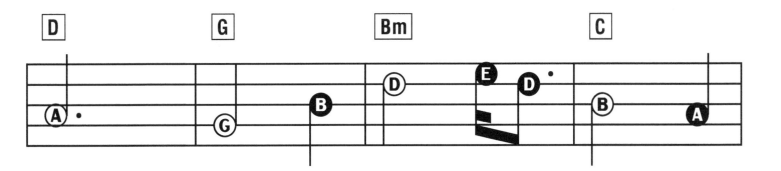

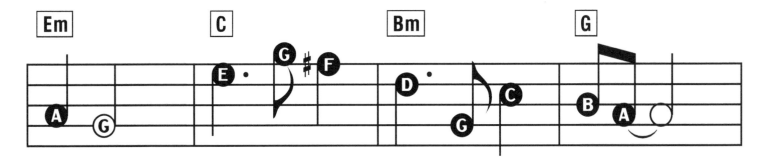

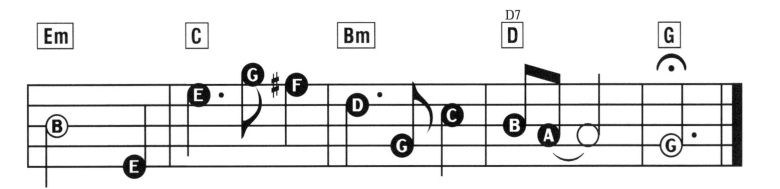

When You're Alone
from the Tristar Motion Picture HOOK

Registration 5
Rhythm: Waltz

Music by John Williams
Lyrics by Leslie Bricusse

When you're all a - lone far a - way from

home, there's a gift the an - gels send when you're a - lone. _____

Ev - 'ry day must end, but the night's our

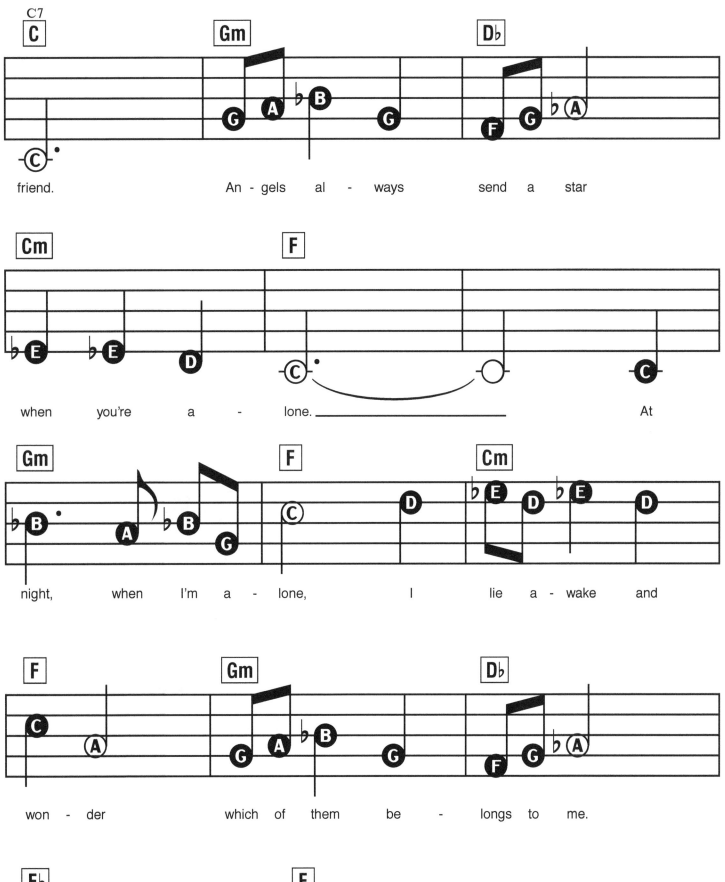

friend.   An - gels al - ways   send   a   star

when   you're   a -   lone. _____   At

night,   when   I'm a - lone,   I   lie   a - wake   and

won - der   which of them   be -   longs   to   me.

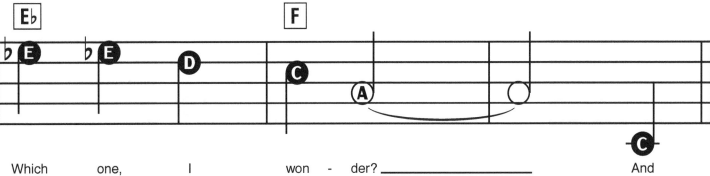

Which   one,   I   won - der? _____   And

an - y   star   I   choose   watch - es   o - ver
stars   are   all   my   friends   till   the   night - time

me.
ends. }   So, I   know   I'm   not   a - lone,

when   I'm   here   on   my   own.   Is - n't   that   a

won - der?   When   you're   a -   lone,   you're   not   a -

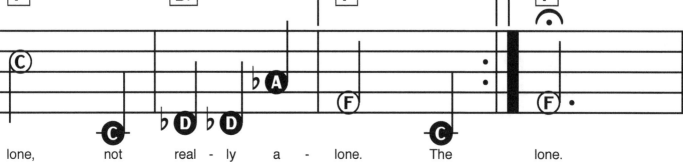

lone,   not   real - ly   a - lone.   The   lone.

Registration Guide

- Match the Registration number on the song to the corresponding numbered category below. Select and activate an instrumental sound available on your instrument.

- Choose an automatic rhythm appropriate to the mood and style of the song. (Consult your Owner's Guide for proper operation of automatic rhythm features.)

- Adjust the tempo and volume controls to comfortable settings.

Registration

1	Mellow	Flutes, Clarinet, Oboe, Flugel Horn, Trombone, French Horn, Organ Flutes
2	Ensemble	Brass Section, Sax Section, Wind Ensemble, Full Organ, Theater Organ
3	Strings	Violin, Viola, Cello, Fiddle, String Ensemble, Pizzicato, Organ Strings
4	Guitars	Acoustic/Electric Guitars, Banjo, Mandolin, Dulcimer, Ukulele, Hawaiian Guitar
5	Mallets	Vibraphone, Marimba, Xylophone, Steel Drums, Bells, Celesta, Chimes
6	Liturgical	Pipe Organ, Hand Bells, Vocal Ensemble, Choir, Organ Flutes
7	Bright	Saxophones, Trumpet, Mute Trumpet, Synth Leads, Jazz/Gospel Organs
8	Piano	Piano, Electric Piano, Honky Tonk Piano, Harpsichord, Clavi
9	Novelty	Melodic Percussion, Wah Trumpet, Synth, Whistle, Kazoo, Perc. Organ
10	Bellows	Accordion, French Accordion, Mussette, Harmonica, Pump Organ, Bagpipes